MORE THAN
REPRESENTATION:

The Cheat Codes to Own Your Seat at the Table

MORE THAN REPRESENTATION:

THE CHEAT CODES TO OWN
YOUR SEAT AT THE TABLE

RAVEN JEMISON

MANUSCRIPTS
PRESS

MORE THAN REPRESENTATION:
The Cheat Codes to Own Your Seat at the Table

ISBN   979-8-88926-794-2 *Paperback*
         979-8-88926-795-9 *Ebook*

To my Ancestors, known and unknown—

*You live in me. I'm eternally grateful
for your endless sacrifice. I humbly
pray that I am making you proud.*

TABLE OF CONTENTS

————

INTRODUCTION

———

I melted at my younger sister's smile as she made her way through our offices. AJay has been my partner-in-crime for as long as I can remember. She is also one of the smartest people I know. To say I was over the moon when she decided to join me at work to shadow Sumathi, our vice president of business strategy and analytics, is an understatement. As a recent graduate from my alma mater, Auburn University, with a degree in finance, AJay had shown an interest in business analytics. So it was a no-brainer for her to learn the ropes at the Milwaukee Bucks; I couldn't wait to hear how the day went.

Not surprisingly, Sumathi raved about how smart and inquisitive AJay was as she asked all the right questions. I was proud. However, I was not quite prepared for what she asked next.

"How did you get to where you are?" my colleague asked.

"What do you mean?" I replied.

"What I mean is you're outspoken, unapologetically authentic, and you have navigated the politics of this male-dominated industry so gracefully. You represent for several marginalized communities so well, and people want to follow you. How did you develop this confidence to stand boldly as yourself while rising in the ranks?"

These were great questions. Ones that I hadn't really thought about in detail. Why *am* I so special? How did a jheri-curled, introverted black kid from Alabama get here and become the representation and manifestation of her ancestors' dreams? Especially a kid who was bullied by other black kids for "acting white," but was also told and shown that she didn't belong in white spaces? What exactly was I representing when people said to me so proudly that "representation matters"?

Sure, I have been asked these questions in some form throughout my entire career. As a high-ranking executive in the competitive, male-dominated sports industry, I am being asked more and more about "The How." How I came to be in this position—my journey, my path, my strategy. Before my conversation with Sumathi that day, I always gave generic responses.

Belief in myself.

Surrounding myself with great people and having them advocate for me.

Working hard.

Right place, right time.

"Blessed and Highly Favored" through divine intervention.

All of those things are right, but they are surface-level answers.

I never addressed the undercurrent of assumption that diversity, equity, inclusion, and belonging (DEIB) efforts had been the sole reason for my being elevated and promoted as a minority employee. In some people's minds, my success was not a result of my work ethic and the value I added to the companies for which I worked, but rather an exception made for my identity.

I didn't discuss the challenges I faced coming out as queer when I already had two strikes against me as a black woman.

I avoided sharing my struggles to climb out of my shell and play the politics necessary to advance up the corporate ladder as my authentic self.

I left the most important pieces out of the story, making it appear easier than it was.

I pretended that the privilege I had as someone in power sheltered me from facing the same obstacles met by others.

The truth is that DEIB efforts have not served ethnic minorities and women of color in the same way they have for white women. Despite my ascension up the ranks, I experienced feelings of being invisible on the journey up. Doubt and fear were still very present.

My answers about how I got here lacked specificity and were not helpful for those charting their paths to the top levels of their careers. I have been blessed to have an abundance of mentees at varying stages in their careers, many of whom were either black, women, and/or queer and first- or second-generation college graduates. Most of them weren't privy to the tools or knowledge necessary to navigate and thrive in spaces that weren't designed for them.

They were me: ill-equipped as the journey began and learning along the way. I have come to realize that I owed it to them and their peers to share the details—good, bad, and ugly. I don't want to just represent for them. I wanted to provide access to the "cheat codes"—the tools and intel necessary to see the path ahead a bit clearer and traverse it a little easier.

After Sumathi's questioning, I spent time thinking about those "cheat codes" and the pieces of the puzzle that made it possible for me to have my current seat at the table.

CHEAT CODE 1: KNOW YOURSELF TO KNOW YOUR WORTH

Before I could provide substantive value to the companies I worked for and be the leader that I knew I could be, I first needed to know who I was. I wanted to remain unapologetically authentic as I made my climb to the top.

CHEAT CODE 2: FIND YOUR PEOPLE

I discovered a circle of friends, family, and colleagues who nurtured and supported every one of my unimaginable dreams. They also corrected and challenged me from a place of love. When my confidence waned, they reminded me who the hell I am.

CHEAT CODE 3: PAUSE, REFLECT, AND REINVEST

The road has been tough, and I almost left the sports industry. But then, I paused to take a breath and refilled my cup with the pieces of joy I needed to find balance. I reflected to assess and celebrate what I had accomplished while adjusting the expectations of perfection I had for myself. Then I reinvested in the skills I needed to continue down the road at the highest level possible.

CHEAT CODE 4: UNDERSTAND THAT POLITICS ISN'T ONLY FOR POLITICIANS

Initially, politics was a game I ran away from, but I finally came to terms with the need to play. But I did it my way. I armed myself with the tools necessary to navigate the spaces not built for me but did so without losing myself in the process.

CHEAT CODE 5: COLLECT ADVOCATES

Advancement in my career was not purely based on meritocracy. It was not only about who I knew, but about who knew me. Along the journey, I found advocates who could speak to my value and contributions even, and especially, when I wasn't in the room.

LEVEL UP: MAKE THE MOST OF YOUR TURN

I wasn't selfish when I got my seat at the table. My goal was and continues to be to leverage my platform and power to make room for others—to call attention to the invisible and speak loud enough for the voiceless.

My journey has not been a straight line. So as you read this book, you'll find that it is not in chronological order. Instead, it's a collection of short stories that make up the pieces of the puzzle that got me here.

I am no longer satisfied with just being a vague representative of what is possible. My responsibility is to be a vessel to learn from.

This book is for the women who feel invisible and voiceless as they struggle to find their seat in the boardroom. It is for the black, indigenous, and people of color (BIPOC) women who sit at the intersection of marginalization and find challenges climbing that proverbial ladder. It is for the queer person who never felt comfortable bringing their full selves to workspaces that weren't designed for them. If you've looked around and felt invisible as everyone else knew exactly what to say, how to dress, or how to fit in to be perfectly comfortable in those spaces, this book is for you.

I will provide you with the cheat codes I learned as I advanced my career in a male-dominated industry. These codes will go deeper than just "keep your head down," "work hard," or "know the right people." I will go beyond being a physical representation of what's possible because, although I believe it matters, I believe access to these cheat codes matter more.

CHAPTER 1:

THE FIRST (TWO) TIME(S)

———

Before we dig in, it's important to set the stage for when I understood the importance of representation and why it mattered. At the very least, I can explain when I contextualized the circumstances that evoked the sentiment.

Two separate occasions spring to memory.

The 1984 Olympics was a pivotal moment for me. Mary Lou Retton was a bubbly, bouncing teenager dominating the gymnastics landscape. My five-year-old self had never seen anything like it. I was mesmerized. I felt a connection. To be honest, I think it was all the winning and celebrating that caught my attention. Nevertheless, I begged my mom to enroll me in gymnastics. Being the ever-supportive parent, she relented and signed me up for Bama Bounders, the University of Alabama's club team.

This was the beginning of something magical for me. I immediately felt at home, challenging my little body to do the things that seemed physically impossible: standing on the four-inch-wide beam, swinging on the bars, and sticking the landing. It's true what they say. Fear is learned. As I advanced from entry level to intermediate, I don't recall feeling any fear as I began my journey as a competitive gymnast. Admittedly, I was *just* okay on the uneven bars, beam, and floor. The vault was my sweet spot. My body was built for the power and speed the vault required.

Let me explain.

I had, and still have, what's called "sprinter's legs." By all accounts, I've had them since birth. As I began to develop as a young adult in my teens, I noticed that my legs were getting bigger and more powerful. Today, strong is the new sexy. Back in the '90s, however, strong for a young female meant I couldn't shop in the girls' section for my clothes, specifically jeans. I had to resort to the boys' section to find jeans that could get over my "thunder thighs." Belts were also my best friend because boys' jeans were too loose in the waist—sigh.

I was envious of girls who could shop in the juniors' section. I recall my first time trying on girls' Guess jeans, a popular denim brand at the time. I was so excited to try on the jeans with their red logo on the right back pocket. But the feeling of discouragement fell over me as I attempted to get the jeans over my knees. I didn't understand. My waist was small. No one prepared me for feeling so out of place in that moment. My mom was also at a loss. When the store clerk knocked on the dressing room door to ask if we were okay, I knew I wasn't. But I needed jeans. My mom asked the clerk what options we had, only to be left with boys' jeans; the ones with the green Guess logo on the right back pocket. There was no hiding from the fact that I was wearing boys' clothes. As a pre-teen trying to fit in, I was devastated.

I hated shopping.

Gymnasts in the 1980s and '90s were not built like me, and they didn't look like me. Mary Lou Retton had gotten my attention, but she was considered the All-American Girl. It didn't take me long to realize that I was far from the stereotype of "All-American." Subsequent Olympic gymnastics teams also featured petite, white girls. So when I looked around at my gymnastics teammates, it was no surprise that I noticed the same. At eleven years old, this was my first foray into that "only" space—or better said, "lonely" space. When I look back at pivotal moments in my life, my experience in gymnastics was one. It prepared me for surviving and thriving as the "only" in more spaces than I care to count.

On occasion, Bama Bounders gymnasts would practice later into the evenings. This would mean a potential crossover with University of Alabama gymnasts. In 1989, on a humid, summer evening in Alabama, my life changed.

As I sat on the floor, stretching and facing the door, I noticed a petite, black gymnast walking into the gym. I did a double take. My attention turned into a gaze as she walked from the door to the locker room. I couldn't describe the feeling I had in that moment, but I now know it as a sense of relief. All the years of feeing alone and invisible as the only black gymnast were suddenly rewarded in a weird way. It was like suffering through eating vegetables for dinner, only to bite into the bowl of ice cream that I'd been thinking about all day; or like all the work I put into getting my driver's license and then, finally, taking my first drive alone or picking up my friends for the first time.

I had a feeling of pure joy.

Dione "Dee Dee" Foster was the first African-American gymnast to receive a scholarship from the University of Alabama. She was a member of the US National team at sixteen, and she was destined for the Olympics. I didn't know any of this at the time. All I knew was that she looked like me, her body was built like mine, and she was a star. When my parents picked me up from practice, my mom also saw Dee Dee and made the connection when she saw the joy on my face. In that moment, I realized the power of representation.

My journey to becoming a world-class gymnast ended at fourteen. I quit for a number of reasons, but I kept my eye on Dee Dee. She became one of the most decorated gymnasts in history for the University of Alabama gymnastics program. That experience was the springboard I needed to know what was possible as "the only."

At the ripe age of fifteen, I turned my attention to college. This was another path with little representation in my personal life. Sure, I'd grown up in the late '80s and '90s, watching *A Different World*, the spin-off from *The Cosby Show*. As Denise Huxtable took her talents to Hillman College—the fictional historic black college/university (HBCU)—and befriended Dwayne and Whitley there, I was glued to the television week after week. Seeing black people thrive in a college setting and being surrounded by examples of black excellence was crucial. I saw myself in them.

Although my mother or my father never finished college, they raised me to value education and the doors it could open for me. They instilled in me that there was only one option: I would not only attend, but I would graduate. Fortunately, my maternal uncle, Andre, was my real-life example as the first person in my family to graduate from college. Hearing of his path was the second instance that I realized the importance of representation and why it mattered. He showed me that getting multiple degrees was possible and reinforced what education could do to break the cycle of poverty and shrink the generational wealth gap.

Andre attended the University of Alabama, a predominately white institution (PWI), and majored in nursing. As I planned my future and zeroed in on what I wanted to be when I grew up, he was a great resource for me. I decided I would pursue optometry as my career choice, and his experiences navigating the collegiate space as a black male came in handy as I applied to schools as a pre-optometry major. Along the way, he shared several stories, many of which mirrored my journey as I got serious about the college application process. One of his stories resonated and infuriated me.

He and I discussed the importance of taking high school advanced placement (AP) classes, particularly in math and science. AP classes were college undergraduate-level courses offered in high schools. Taking these courses and acing their respective exams offered at the end of the school year had several advantages. I focused on the potential for college credits and boosts to my GPA.

My senior year, I enrolled in AP Chemistry with Mrs. Alexander, the same teacher who coincidentally taught my uncle. I knew it would be a challenge, but I was ready. Or so I thought. I struggled early in the class. The pace was fast, and I was too prideful to ask for help. When I did, she left much to be desired in her way of assistance. During a parent-teacher conference, she told my parents that science wasn't a strong subject for me, and I should consider dropping the course. As a point of reference, she was also the same teacher I had when I aced regular chemistry. At the time, I wasn't sure why she would tell my mom this knowing that I'd been successful in her class previously. Feeling sad and discouraged, I told my uncle what she said through a face full of tears. It's kind of hard to become a doctor if you're not good at science. I believed what she told me. But what he told me next lit a fire under me that still burns bright today.

When Andre was a nursing student at the University of Alabama in the '80s, he struggled with a math course. The response from his academic counselor was not a shock, but it was disheartening nonetheless.

"In my sophomore year, I had to take an Introduction to Statistics class as a prerequisite. Knowing that I was good at core math, algebra, calculus, and so on, I decided to take a class that was more challenging for me," he said.

My uncle was my hero. Usually when he spoke I listened intently, trying to absorb all his gems of wisdom. At this moment, however, I wasn't in the mood for a story. I wanted to engage as best I could despite my dejection, but all I could muster was a nod in response.

He continued. "I had a hard time grasping the concepts right away, despite studying for endless hours alone and with my study group. I got a D on my first test, but I didn't let it deter me. It never occurred to me to quit or drop the class. I went to my counselor for my early semester check in and discussion on my courses for the following semester. She asked how my classes were going. I casually mentioned that the statistics class was a challenge and that I made a D on my first test. Her response was that I should reconsider nursing as my major if I'm having a hard time in math."

I perked up and immediately interrupted him. "You're not bad at math. You love math. If it weren't for you, there's no way I would have aced Algebra III last year," I replied. Andre was a math whiz, and I often accepted his tutoring for some of my challenging math classes in high school.

He replied, "I know I'm not bad at math. Confused as to why her first reaction was for me to abandon my major altogether, I asked why she said that. Her response wasn't surprising, but still jarring. 'Sometimes courses, like math and science, can be difficult for black people.' I wasn't surprised because I'd heard that before, but I was jarred when it rolled out of her mouth so quickly."

I was stunned. Obviously, I was aware that people felt this way. I believe my surprise came from her gall to say it. This was the '80s, not the '50s or '60s. And here I am in the late '90s hearing the same thing from my teacher.

Instead of providing Andre with tools and resources to improve his chances of success in the course, she told him he should consider another major. The trope that blacks weren't good in math and science guided her counseling. His advice to me wasn't to go on and on about something or someone he couldn't control. He made it clear that his intention from that moment on was to prove her wrong. He not only went on to get a bachelor's degree in nursing, but another bachelor's in mechanical engineering and a master's degree in nursing.

A piece of me thinks he collected degrees specifically because of what this counselor said to him.

As he told me this story, I remember feeling that this was going to be the norm for me. By sharing his experience, our bond grew stronger. I had someone who I could look to then and now when I have to prove people wrong as "the only one." His guidance, counseling, and "representation" of what was possible pushed me to dig deep to prove Mrs. Alexander wrong.

I studied like I'd never studied before and chose to use her "advice" as fuel.

I aced AP Chemistry.

I saw Dee Dee Foster and my uncle Andre succeed in spaces that weren't built for them. These were two shining examples of "firsts" thriving. But what was in the undercurrent? They presented themselves as ducks on the water; gliding beautifully through life, but peddling furiously through the murky, messy underbelly of misogyny, racism, and classism.

There was more to the story.

CHEAT CODE 1:

KNOW YOURSELF TO KNOW YOUR WORTH

The energy it takes to be someone else is exhausting.

Before I could provide substantive value to the companies I worked for and be the leader I knew I could be, I first needed to know who I was. I wanted to remain unapologetically authentic as I made my climb to the top.

In the first cheat code, you'll learn about the winding road on the path to becoming me. This includes the self-hatred and struggles I had coming out as a gay woman with ambitions of making it to the C-suite and the internal challenges I faced on my natural hair journey. All of this is necessary as passage through to the other side of accepting myself and celebrating the gifts that make me uniquely me. Once I discovered that my uniqueness was my superpower, I leveraged that as the value that only I could offer any company that hired me.

If I didn't define myself for myself, I would be crunched into other people's fantasies for me and eaten alive.

—AUDRE LORDE

CHAPTER 2:

IDENTITY

———

My birthday is July 31. Whenever I mention that to someone familiar with astrology, their first response is usually, "Ohhhh, you're a Leo!" To which, I immediately respond, "I'm not *really*" to rebuke the notion that I bask in the spotlight and crave attention as all Leos do. After all, I was the introverted kid who was bullied by black kids for "acting white," and I felt alone in white spaces. I always felt alone and invisible. It couldn't be further from the truth to say I wanted to be in the limelight and have all eyes on me.

My perspective changed after one speaking engagement.

As executive vice president of business operations for the Milwaukee Bucks, I'm often asked to speak to aspiring sports professionals. Early in my tenure at the Bucks, I was asked to speak on a panel for the SheBelieves Summit. The summit is US Soccer's commitment to empower young women and girls while continuing to grow women's soccer in the United States and across the globe. Attendees were a select group of women who were college-aged students and young professionals. The goal was to provide them with the opportunity to learn from and network with industry professionals.

I squeezed this engagement into my schedule—I was in and out of Los Angeles within twenty-four hours. After leaving the stage, I headed to grab a quick lunch with the attendees before rushing off to catch my flight back to Milwaukee. As I stood in line for the buffet, I looked across the room and saw a black female staring through me. She was standing next to the table along with a couple of other students. I waved awkwardly and proceeded to grab my plate. I headed in the direction of their table, and the look on her face was one of nervous excitement. She asked if I would join her and her friends for lunch. Never the cool kid growing up, I met her emotion with a smile and sat down.

I should probably lay out how I typically handle these situations. I'm often bombarded with requests for mentorship, résumé reviews, and "five minutes to pick my brain." LinkedIn has created avenues for up-and-coming professionals to dive deep into your experience to establish a connection. Truthfully, I wish I had LinkedIn when I was coming of age in the sports business industry. However, because little is taught on how to move a connection online to a live conversation in a networking setting, the interactions are often awkward. Picture rambling conversations with no elevator pitch in sight, and an ask for all the secrets about how to get in the industry. I try not to judge. I remember how I got my start. I was not polished, and I had no idea how to make myself stand out among the others. Knowing how that one interaction could have changed the trajectory of my life, I push through the awkwardness to make eye contact and give sports career hopefuls my undivided attention.

I assumed the encounter with this woman would be much of the same. I was wrong.

Before I could put my plate down, she proceeded to tell me that she had been following me since her freshman year. She wrote a paper on my career in her freshman English Composition class. With tears in her eyes, she shared that she was also a queer woman. Her tears became uncontrollable sobbing. After collecting herself, she thanked me for being an example of what's possible for a black queer woman ascending the ranks in spaces not built for us.

A flurry of emotions rushed through me as I listened to this woman share her story unabashedly. I was speechless, embarrassed, proud, grateful, and moved. What she didn't know was that I often felt invisible and overlooked, and she was giving to me what I had given to her: the feeling of being seen.

We proceeded to talk about similarities between the two of us. Most notably that we were the second person in our respective families to go to college. She didn't have connections in the industry. She wasn't attending an Ivy League school, which evoked concerns about getting a job in a competitive industry after college. She was me twenty years ago. No one told me how to get a job in sports. I didn't have any connections. But here I was, sitting in the C-suite of a multibillion-dollar organization. I thought sharing my story via podcasts and articles was good enough. Just sitting in the seat at the proverbial table was good enough and my work was done. Right?

I've been in this industry for seventeen years and have had too many of these conversations to remember. However, it was this moment when I realized that I was to her what Dee Dee Foster and my uncle Andre were to me. I was the peek behind the curtain. I was her beacon of light. I was no longer the person who believed it was just my hard work that got me here. Sure, I busted my ass to get two degrees and add value to the teams I've worked for—studying late and often, working ungodly long hours, sacrificing relationships. But it was a disservice to stop there when telling my story.

We owe it to the next generation to be truthful about the journey. Truthful about the joy and the pain, about the wins and losses, about the fears and courage, and about the twists and turns that made the journey worthwhile. Andre and Dee Dee were the epitome of what we call "Black Excellence" today. But there was more to their story. I never spoke to Dee Dee about her journey and my uncle passed away before we could discuss the level of successes in my career that brought both joy and pain.

Was Dee Dee ever told she should consider another sport other than gymnastics because her body was better suited for, say, track? My gymnastics coach told me that, and it put doubt into my mind as an already confused, twelve-year-old kid—a kid who was already struggling with body image issues as she battled puberty. If Dee Dee was discouraged during her career, how did she handle it? How did she push through the discouragement and become the gymnast who excelled at the University of Alabama, a predominately white institution in the Heart of Dixie? Was she ever called "too white" because she valued an education and the doors it would open for her to see more than what was in front of her? I was, and it shaped my formative years. Never cool enough to hang with my black peers, but too black to be welcomed into the white circles other than in the classroom.

My uncle changed careers from nursing to get a degree in mechanical engineering. This meant his work setting changed from a hospital dealing with patients to being in corporate boardrooms with prospective clients. Did he mute his "Southern" accent to a more neutral one, so he wouldn't be met with the "slow and ignorant" trope? Did he go home exhausted every single day from not being able to show emotion like his white colleagues for fear of being seen as difficult to work with or the "angry black man"? This is called code switching, a strategy for black people to successfully navigate interracial interactions that has large implications on their well-being, economic advancement, and even physical survival (McCluney 2021).

Yes, I've had to *code switch*. "Don't be the 'angry black woman,' be likable. Don't be intimidating, look respectable. Don't look too gay and maybe you'll have a chance at a level playing field." Those are the other full-time jobs that I, and members of many marginalized communities, have to hold alongside our day jobs.

Hearing that this young woman was facing the same challenges I faced two decades ago revealed something to me. Her seeing me in the seat was not enough. In her words, it was great to see me here, but she wanted to know the "how." This encounter uncovered something deeper. My goal shouldn't be just to show what's possible on the surface. To make the most of my platform, I needed to share what it took to navigate the various access points or service roads, such that I could help make their journey smoother. Most importantly, I needed to be clear that it wasn't easy, which was also a good thing. Struggles in the short term were only obstacles and challenges to be conquered. Through those struggles, I gained tools in my arsenal to help me overcome adversity. Looking back, adversity was a gift, even though it didn't feel like it while I was going through it.

One of those points of adversity on my journey was the struggle to find and define my identity.

Admittedly, I had no idea who I was when entering the sports industry in 2006. The life I was building up to that point was not the life that matched my passions. I'd forsaken years of preparation for optometry school to pursue a career in sports with full force. Although I didn't know who I was, I knew what I was: driven, ambitious, and determined to prove I belonged. We'll get back to that word "belong" later.

When I stepped into my first role as an entry-level sales representative for the National Hockey League's Florida Panthers, I did so with little hesitation that I would work harder and longer than the next person. In those early months, I wasn't focused on climbing the ladder or being the boss. Don't get me wrong, I eyed the C-suite and corner offices as I walked to my cubicle each day. But early on, I knew my journey would go nowhere if I didn't prove myself in my current role. I just wanted to win.

I not only won at sales, but I also stood out. Within seven months of starting, I was promoted to a newly created role and unknowingly began that trek up the ladder. Things were clicking at work, and I loved the pressure. The pressure of having to "sell to eat" in South Florida was real. I was gaining exposure to the leaders in the organization and making a name for myself as someone who would get stuff done.

As I reflect on that time now, however, it was arguably one of the most painful times in my life. I was disconnected from the "real me" and using work to block out the noise. I had no clue who I was.

Let me take a minute to clarify what I mean here.

Two beautiful souls and a village raised me, instilling the values of a what a good human should be. Growing up in the Deep South, I learned these values as early as I could talk: be kind, do what you say you'll do, make eye contact when you speak to someone, respect your elders, do unto others as you'll have them do unto you, and so on. I attempted to lead with those tenets every day, and I knew what I stood for. Integrity and identity are two different things. When I talk about not knowing who I was at this time in my life, I'm talking about my identity as an individual and how I wanted to be seen out in the world.

In 2007, as I was being lauded for "crushin' it" at work, I was lost. As a member of the lesbian, gay, bisexual, transgender, queer or questioning, intersex, asexual, and more (LGBTQIA+) community, coming out was a monumental moment. I had not come out to anyone beyond a few close friends. I was buried in the closet, and I had not mustered up the courage to come out in any larger sense. As a child of the South's Bible Belt, it was particularly challenging as I battled many of the teachings I'd learned growing up. Without turning this into a religious book, I'll just say the Bible, as I was taught, had me destined to hell.

A few years earlier, I attempted to come out to my mom. I was in a relationship at the time and wanted her to know about it. I've never been good at lying or keeping things from her. But I had reached a breaking point. I also just wanted her to know that I was happy. I wrote down the words exactly as I would say them in the hopes that it would help me say the right thing for her. I needed her to hear me clearly with no confusion of the message. Just saying "I'm gay," didn't feel right. As I sat her down on the couch in my apartment, I read what was on the paper, word for word. I was so nervous that I had my head down and focused on the paper the entire time, not wanting to see the look on her face. As I finished, I looked up and saw her face covered in tears.

Silence.

She sat there crying and shaking her head "no" for what felt like hours. When she finally spoke, all she asked was "Are you sure?" to which I said "yes."

She got up and walked out of my apartment to her car. I followed her. With tears in her eyes, she started the car, said "I love you," and drove away. As the daughter of a Pentecostal preacher, she too lived and breathed the teachings that being gay was a first class, one-way ticket to hell. She didn't say it at the time, but I know the tears were out of concern for my soul.

That experience of rejection was so traumatic. I went back into the closet—all the way back in.

In my mind, living "out and proud" was not possible. I wanted to shrink into the darkest corners of my mind, hide out, and just pour myself into my work. I was already a hard worker, but this was when the real "workaholic" in me was born. I was hiding from truly loving myself and fully living as myself.

As if being gay wasn't enough to deal with, I was also early in my dreadlocks (locs) journey.

As a black woman, my hair is *not just hair*. It represents pride, struggle, love, and pain. Thinking back to my childhood, it was also symbolic of the times sitting in the beauty shop listening to the wisdom of older black women. They owned these spaces, literally and figuratively. As a young girl, I didn't always understand the conversations, but I recognized the community they built and the expressions exhibited. The joy that resonated throughout the shop was palpable and beautiful to witness.

The not-so-beautiful parts of having my hair, our hair, is that it's often policed as a source of discrimination, used as a weapon in the respectability politics game, and too often misunderstood. Long after I began the journey of loving my hair, an official campaign to end hair discrimination was started. In 2019, Dove and the CROWN Coalition in partnership with then-State Senator Holly J. Mitchell of California created the CROWN (Creating a Respectful and Open World for Natural Hair) Act. According to the Dove CROWN research study in 2023, over 20 percent of black women surveyed—twenty-five to thirty-four black women—were sent home from the workplace because of their hair. Black women with coily/textured hair are two times as likely to experience microaggressions in the workplace than black women with straight hair (CROWN Coalition 2023).

Unfortunately for me, the CROWN Act was not around in 2006 as I began my career. The beginning of my locs journey coincided with my start in sports. During that time, I heard and experienced many hurtful things, often from black people.

"You'll never get a 'real job' with locs."

"You won't be taken seriously. You're already a black woman. Why would you add more on your plate to overcome?"

"If you want to grow your career in sports, you'll need more executive presence."

"What are you doing with your hair?"

"Can I touch it?"

It was a dagger to the soul to hear some of these comments from black people. But I couldn't blame them. Their intentions were good, but their comments were a reflection of the complex, nuanced systems we navigate as we fight to be respected and "good enough." Comments like this from those outside the black community, however, were reminders of the toxicities of those complex systems.

I struggled. I was living my dream on the surface, with no tether to who I was below. I knew if I didn't take control of my internal narrative, then external forces would tell my story for me. They would control how the world saw me and conformity would be the tool I would lean on to get up the corporate ladder. Despite having two more strikes against me, I was determined to make sure that didn't happen. I was now on the journey to not only finding who I am, but also own and take up space as me.

CHAPTER 3:

THE VICTORY OF INTERSECTIONALITY. THE AGONY OF DIVERSITY.

———

Acceptance is a gift I often give to others, without a second thought of giving it to myself.

At times, the journey toward accepting all the pieces of me was a lonely one. It was accompanied by equal parts hard work and hard truths about how I wanted to show up in the world. One step at a time, one day at a time, I attempted to make peace with the fact that I couldn't control how people viewed me as a black woman. I slowly began to understand that I was born gay, and despite what I'd been taught growing up in the church, it wasn't a choice. I looked in the mirror each morning, styled my growing locs, and thought about the black women in the beauty shop from my youth. There wasn't a "one-size-fits-all" hairstyle that made those women beautiful. They were all different. I began reading books about the black women who were political and civil rights activists from the mid-1900s. There was no such thing as a monolithic black woman. So why am I trying to fit into this box that I and others have created for me?

Positive affirmations became my second language. *I am a queer, black woman, and I can only be the best "me" I can be.*

This is who I am. It's not all I am, and it's not all I'll ever be. There will be many iterations of me as I evolve and continue to work on being the best version I can be. But at the core, I awakened to the possibility that I could impact and influence those who look and love like me only as the true version of me. Intersectionality was my gift to myself and others. I sat in gratitude of all my "otherness."

Acceptance of myself was the first step. It was a pivotal moment. An overwhelming level of joy and peace accompanied this moment. It's hard to explain as there has yet to be a point in my life that has replicated it. I slowly unburdened myself from the pressures of society to truly accept myself as me. Over time, I embraced my younger self as she tried to conform to the "All-American" standards of being a gymnast. I told her she no longer had to shrink to make room for others. The person she is today is grateful for the challenges we faced because it created the calluses needed to forge through unwelcoming spaces.

The second step on my journey was coming out at work and proudly living my life as a queer woman.

My career was blossoming as I took on a new sales leadership role with the Pittsburgh Pirates. My locs had grown to shoulder length, and I proudly wore them as the crown they were designed to be. On the surface, Pittsburgh was not an apparent and booming LGBTQIA+ oasis. I was in a long-distance relationship at the time, making it even more difficult. I failed at balancing love, the new job, new colleagues, and a new city. My relationship suffered and eventually ended. Although devastating, it bought me some time to figure out how to come out to my colleagues at the Pirates. But I was still miserable.

In true type A fashion, I focused on what I could control—which was drowning myself in work.

A year passed, and I was burned out. I needed an outlet, so I had the courage to join an online dating service. The year was 2011. I met April, the most amazing human. I fell head over heels. This was it! But I was still in the closet, which meant that it wasn't really *it*, unless I could tell someone. But who?

In my first year at the Pirates, I developed friendships with several of my colleagues and their wives. I clicked with Danielle, one of the wives, and formed what I thought was a trusted bond. She also worked in sports, so I thought she could also provide perspective on what being "out" in the industry could mean for me. One evening, we went out for happy hour, and I confided in her. I was nervous because other than to my mom, I hadn't really said the words, "I'm gay." But I was in love, so I winged it.

We sat down at the bar, and I immediately asked for a shot of tequila. After some small talk, I went in. "So, I have something to tell you, but I'm not exactly sure how," I said.

"What's going on?" she replied as she turned her attention to me as we'd both been focused on the TV in the bar showing the Pittsburgh Penguins game.

I guzzled the shot and replied, "I'm dating someone."

She perked up and said, "Oh my god! That's so great. Tell me about him. What does he do? How did you meet him?"

I'd never zoned in so much on a pronoun as much as I did in that conversation. It seemed like she said he or him a billion times!

Without even thinking, I said, "*She* is a dancer, and *she* lives in Buffalo. *Her* name is April. We met on eHarmony and *she's* coming to Pittsburgh this weekend. I'd love for you to meet *her*."

Whew. Here we go.

Without batting an eye, Danielle replied, "That is awesome! I'm so happy for you. I can't wait to meet her."

I immediately felt lighter. Danielle asked a few more questions about April, before agreeing on a date and time to meet April during her upcoming visit. I went home that evening ready to conquer the world. I had passed the test. And it was much easier than I thought. I asked Danielle not to share it with her husband, Justin. He was a colleague of mine, and I needed to muster up the courage to do so myself. She agreed.

A couple of days later, I set an end-of-day meeting with Justin to share my news.

I was still high off the night with Danielle, so I was ready to go when he walked in. "You're probably wondering why I set this meeting at the end of the day. I'd like to share something with you."

Justin's body language shifted as though I was about to tell him he won the lottery. He said, casually but giddy, "What's up?"

"I told Danielle this already, but I'm gay and I'm dating a woman named April who lives in Buffalo." To this day, I'm not sure why I was so formal about it. Nonetheless, it was done. I was out.

"I know," he replied as he shifted from a pensive posture to a more welcoming one.

I was taken aback. What did he mean? Had I not been as careful as I thought? All kind of crazy stuff started going through my head. Shocked, I asked, "What do you mean you know?"

"Danielle told me," he said.

I was speechless, angry, and devastated. "How the f*&$ could she do this to me?" I thought.

But what happened next was the most beautiful experience: Justin walked to where I was sitting and gave me the biggest hug. "I support you and am here for whatever you need. Thank you for trusting me to tell me this," he said.

He went on to ask questions about April and actively listened to the answers. I went home that night and cried like a baby—tears of joy and relief. Even though I was outed by Danielle—sidebar: never out someone—I felt empowered. It was that interaction that shattered all the doubt of who I could be moving forward. I also began caring less about what people thought about me. April began joining me at company events, and those closest to me welcomed her. To this day, she continues to be everyone's favorite.

I never went back into the closet.

I realized this acceptance also made me a happier, more productive employee and a better leader. I can't say I no longer have to code-switch or I never have bad days. I will say that after I came out, the view from where I was sitting was no longer clouded with the dread of balancing the "work me" and the "home me." I realized embracing the intersections in which I sit are not only valuable to me, they're also valuable to any organization that's lucky to have me.

As I've grown in my career, I've attempted to stay true to the fact that authentically showing up as my full self is a win for all. However, with the emphasis on "diversity" for companies, those wins aren't always equal—and they can oftentimes come off as disingenuous.

Each year, the Institute for Diversity and Ethics in Sport (TIDES) does a comprehensive analysis of the hiring practices of Major League Baseball (MLB), the National Basketball Association (NBA), the Women's National Basketball Association (WNBA), the National Football League (NFL), Major League Soccer (MLS), and College Sport. This analysis is known as the Racial and Gender Report Card. The 2022 report card was published at a critical moment; it was the mirror, so to speak, on the effect of two years of diversity, equity, and inclusion practices that flooded every industry in our country following the murder of George Floyd.

For racial hiring practices, the WNBA and NBA received an A+, and MLS got an A. The NFL earned a B+, and MLB got a B. College Sport came in last with a C. MLB and the NBA increased by 3.8 percent and 2.2 percent from the previous year, respectively. Conversely, WNBA, NFL, MLS, and College Sport decreased 5.7 percent, 3.5 percent, 0.9 percent, and 1.1 percent, respectively (Lapchick 2022, 3). On the surface, however, this was positive news.

Below the surface in my world of sports business, however, diversity is lacking. Sporting roles like general managers and head coaches skew the data. When looking at my ultimate destination of president/CEO—those who make decisions on the business—the results are less positive and representation is lacking. The percentage of white presidents/CEOs in the MLB is 92.3 percent, 93 percent in the NBA, 81.3 percent in the NFL, 83.3 percent in the WNBA, and 82.1 percent in MLS (Lapchick 2022, 8, 12, 16, 20). When discussing gender diversity in the ranks, it's worse, with the exception of the WNBA with 75 percent of teams being led by women (Lapchick 2022, 25).

After the summer of 2020 and the murders of George Floyd, Breonna Taylor, and Ahmaud Arbery, the calls for black lives to matter were ear piercing. What followed was more action and less talk for more diverse voices to be included in the conversations in the corporate world, including the sports industry. With the statistics above, the industry took notice that there was work to do to increase diversity in key leadership roles.

In 2020, I was working for the National Basketball Association's Team Marketing and Business Operations group. I was being groomed to take the next step as a C-suite executive at a sports team. I received an influx of calls from recruiters and headhunters who had never reached out to me before. Suddenly, they were peddling the "next and best" role for me as a leader in the C-suite.

Concurrently, as I was getting those calls, I also heard rumblings from nonminorities saying they would never be able to get a job again.

I brushed those rumblings aside until I had a conversation with a former colleague, Robert, in late 2020. A leadership role was vacant at a team.

"Raven, did you see that the Dallas Mavericks have a chief revenue officer role open?" Robert asked.

"Yes, I saw that," I replied.

"Are you interested in going back to the team side? That would be a great role for you. You should put your name in the hat," he said. His demeanor was weird, and he had a passive-aggressive tone, but it was also as if he was having a conversation with someone he didn't know. Obligatory would be the best way to describe it.

"No thanks. I'm good. I'm really enjoying my time here at the league. I'm not ready to go back to a team just yet," I replied, sensing that there was something behind his questioning.

"Really? It's as good a time as any. You should strike while the iron is hot!" he said.

"What does that mean?" I asked. At this point, I was getting annoyed because I had a feeling where this conversation was going. I didn't want to believe it, so I tried to give him the benefit of the doubt.

"You know what I mean. It's just a good time for you to have your name out there," he replied with a Cheshire cat grin on his face.

I was officially pissed now. But I wanted to hear him say it. "I'm sorry. I don't understand," I said.

He started fumbling over his words. I could see him thinking about what was coming out of his mouth. "It's just that with diversity being the top priority for teams, I think you'd have a really good shot at getting it," he said.

"Are you saying that the need for diversity is the only reason I would get it? Because I check several boxes?" I angrily replied.

"No, no, no. I'm just saying that they would never consider me. My chances of getting roles like that are over," he said.

Boom! There it was! I couldn't believe it, but I could all at the same time. He was saying the quiet part out loud. According to him, I was a great fit for it—but not for the reasons I should have been. This conversation was burned in my brain. It's reminiscent of the feeling I had during conversations about affirmative action. According to the powers that be, I couldn't get that job based on merit. It had to be because I checked so many diversity boxes that I would be a slam dunk.

All the work I did to know and accept me as *me* mattered most during interactions like this, and there have been too many to count at this point. The microaggressions that existed in everyday conversations within corporate America were exhausting and great reminders. For me, I dialed back into the early days of not knowing myself and the feeling of not wanting others to define how I showed up in the workplace and in interactions like this.

I reminded myself of the work I have done and the value I have added to companies, not just because I'm diverse, but because I've proven my value. I worked tirelessly to prove I could contribute to both the top and bottom lines of an organization.

The bottom line is my intersectional identity is my superpower. I am no one's checked box.

CHAPTER 4:

AUTHENTICALLY MEETING THE MOMENT

———

As my path up the corporate ladder continued, I was in pursuit of that elusive authenticity and not checked boxes. I wanted to show up at work and in professional settings as the person who was comfortable in her own skin. I was always a private person who believed my work life and personal life should never intertwine. I believed the more I shared about myself and my emotions, the more I would be seen as a "weak" and "emotional" leader. As a woman in business, that was the "kiss of death."

However, after I came out during my tenure at the Pirates, I developed real friendships with several of my colleagues. I believed if I surrounded myself with people who supported me, I could take the small steps toward living an "out and proud" existence at work. Don't get me wrong. I wasn't walking around the office in a Love is Love shirt, draped in a rainbow flag. It was gradual. I only let a few people in.

My mom was the only one left in my world who hadn't come to terms with the fact that I was a black, queer woman. After I met April, I was convinced I could no longer hide my happiness. My friends could see the difference in me as my relationship blossomed. I had to temper that in conversations with my mom. As my best friend, she was the one I shared everything with—except this. To live in my full truth, I had to attempt another "coming out" with her. I knew once my Mom met April, she would fall in love with her as I had.

When I was living in Pittsburgh, April was in Buffalo, which was forty-five minutes from Niagara Falls. My mom always wanted to see the Falls, so I thought I would lump all the stress of my "second coming out" with a trip to see this great wonder and meet my new girlfriend. Looking back on it, this was a hell of a risky proposition. It could have gone tragically wrong.

I don't recall ever saying to my mom—again—that I was gay, but I do remember saying I was happy. On one phone call, she asked how I was doing. My response was "I'm doing really well. I met someone. Her name is April."

My mom's response was: "Really. That's good."

Although I was shocked, I didn't bat an eye as I jumped into telling her who April was—infectious spirit, dancer, choreographer, double-lung transplant recipient living with cystic fibrosis. I went on and on, but I ended with "I want you to meet her."

The moment of silence felt like a lifetime.

"Okay," she replied.

"Great. She lives in Buffalo, which is a short drive from Niagara Falls. We can take a drive up to visit her and bring her along on our visit to the Falls," I said.

"Okay. Sounds good," she said.

Four years had passed since my first attempt at coming out. I never really asked my mother what work she did to come to terms with who I was, but I didn't want to press. I just wanted to accept this as a victory.

On the three-hour drive from Pittsburgh to Buffalo, my mom and I carried on as if nothing transformative was about to commence. I loved "road tripping" with my mom, but deep down, I was nervous. I knew better than to open a dialogue about what was about to happen. We talked about everything other than her meeting my new girlfriend.

We pulled up to the duplex on Irving Place, where April lived. What happened next still gives me goosebumps and brings tears to my eyes.

April ran out and ran straight to my mom with her arms open wide. My mom didn't bat an eye and reciprocated. I took the deepest breath I have ever taken at their embrace. Their bond from that moment on has only gotten stronger.

This was the turning point and the final piece to the puzzle of me living in my truth. I shut the door to the proverbial closet forever.

My confidence grew as I began to show up at work differently. I was still a relatively private person. However, I found that I cared less about what people thought of me, and I spent more time growing my skills as a leader. With the stress of hiding pieces of myself gone, I could focus on what it was going to take for me to climb the ladder.

As my career blossomed with stints at the NFL's San Francisco 49ers and the NBA's League Office, I continued to be the "only one." I was the only black person, the only queer person, and/or the only woman in leadership. I took the responsibility seriously. Anything I did would be a reflection on all the communities I represented. I relished in the fact that if I did things the right way, then I could open the door for others to sit at the table.

All that said, I never wanted the spotlight. I just wanted to "do the work."

After my tenure at the NBAleague office, I was blessed with an opportunity to serve as executive vice president of business operations for the Milwaukee Bucks. I went from being a relatively nondescript executive at the League Office to the number two for one of its franchises. I spent six years honing my strategy-building and business operations chops to being held accountable for a business's successes and failures. I thought I was ready.

Let me clarify.

I was more than ready to take on this new challenge and boldly lead the largest team I'd ever led. But despite being comfortable in who I was and what I brought to the table, little prepared me for the thrust "out of the shadows" and into the spotlight. I wasn't ready for the attention. I knew that as a black woman at this level, the LinkedIn connection requests, "hire me" inquiries, and countless "pick my brain" invitations would increase. But the podcast interviews, article features, industry awards, and panels were too much of the gate.

The stage lights were bright—too bright.

I'm not complaining. I know this is par for the course. I just did not know it would happen as quickly as it did. And it happened before I felt I had proved anything in my role. I was just getting started. I wasn't exactly sure why all these people wanted to talk to me or feature me. I have been and will always be a "team-first" leader. As I was doing these appearances, I felt inauthentic. I was putting on a show because I took this role, but I hadn't yet proven myself.

It was weird.

The notoriety was overwhelming. I was embarrassed. I wanted it to stop. After receiving *Adweek*'s Most Powerful Women in Sports award, I shared my annoyance with one of my colleagues, Kareeda. I was looking for sympathy or at least empathy. The conversation that ensued changed me forever.

"Congratulations, Raven," Kareeda said.

"Thank you. But I'm not sure I deserve this. I just got here. I don't want my teammates to think that *this* is what I'm here for," I replied.

"What? Girl, this isn't about you," she said bluntly.

"Um, okay," I said nervously.

"This is about the people who look like us but don't see women like us at the top. There are so few black women leading sports teams. So few queer women in leadership in professional sports. This is the power of representation," she said.

There goes that word again: *representation*.

But what I also heard was *responsibility*. I couldn't shrink into the background. Instead, I could showcase that people who looked like me and loved like me could sit in the seat of power. The story of my humble yet ambitious beginnings needed to be told, but more than anything, it needed to be heard. Someone needed to see that we could accomplish more than just dribbling or running with a ball. First- and second-generation college students needed evidence of what can happen when you intently focus on a dream.

She was right. This was not about me.

I stood corrected, but humbly grateful. I simply replied, "You're right. Thank you for that."

After that conversation, I was no longer thinking of these opportunities as I had been. I became more intentional about how I showed up. If this level of exposure was something I had to get used to, I also had to do so living it out with confidence. I had to meet the moment so those watching can place a higher value on what you can become when you lead with authenticity.

I started to align my responsibility at this level with my purpose. My responsibility was to be "out and about" speaking to people on a larger stage. My purpose was serving with intention. Before each interaction, appearance, or podcast, I always prayed my words would have the impact I intended. I never want it to be "look at me." Instead, my purpose was to show that it's possible to not only survive, but thrive as your authentic self.

In 2022, I had a chance to really put this purpose to the test.

Professional Dimensions, a Milwaukee-based women's professional development organization, was putting on its annual signature event, the Ideation Summit. I received an email from the CEO of the organization—also my sorority sister—announcing their headliner for the event: Tunde Oyeneyin. Tunde—*New York Times* best-selling author of *SPEAK*, Nike athlete, Peloton cycling instructor, and all-around *force of nature*—was hands down one of my favorite Peloton instructors. Her ability to motivate, draw out emotions and sometimes tears, and inspire was unlike anything I've experienced during an exercise class. It was spiritual.

Also in the email was a request for me to partner with another local female executive for a moderated fireside chat with Tunde. I didn't think twice. Despite the fact that I'd never interviewed anyone on stage, I was pumped.

I prepared for this interview as Oprah would—or at least how I thought she would. I read Tunde's book, *SPEAK*, and I studied her Instagram page. I took her classes in the lead up to the interview. I wanted to be seen as a serious moderator and not the "fan girl" I really was.

But then, I panicked. As I delved into her social media persona, I saw someone who "oozed" fashion. She was also a makeup artist in her former life, which meant her face was always "beat" as the kids say.

Doubt began creeping in.

I would hardly describe myself as a fashionista. I prioritize comfort and sneakers over style most days, mostly due to a plethora of injuries resulting from my former life as an athlete. That said, I grew up in an industry where I was and continue to be surrounded by people in suits and ties. I conformed to the "way one should dress" when meeting with a client, walking around the office, or even on the big stage. In the weeks before our interview with Tunde, I agonized over what to wear knowing that I would be sitting/standing next to someone who exhibited so much confidence and *shine*. Mind you, this was also a conference for professional women. In my mind, I had to play the part.

I proceeded to dig into the back corners of my closet to retrieve the corporate uniform: a blazer, blouse, and heel combination. The heels were necessary because there was no way I would be the shorty in any of the pictures with Tunde. I had to *pop* standing next to this woman. Never mind how uncomfortable I would be as I tucked my broad shoulders into the blazer and my surgically-repaired Achilles into the high heels.

Fast-forward to the morning of the event.

I made a last minute decision to prioritize comfort. So I ditched the blazer and blouse and went with a sportier leather jacket. But conformity was still holding court. I brought the heels because I had to stick to some version of the "uniform." I did walk into the event wearing a pair of sneakers—Jordan 1 Lows to be specific. We met Tunde and, of course, she looked stunning in an all-blue suit and a red lipstick that would make Rhianna jealous. Ten minutes before we went on stage, I grabbed my heels, untied my shoes, and something just clicked with a litany of thoughts running through my head.

"Wait a minute. Who am I trying to impress?"

"Why am I so concerned about what people are going to think of me if I don't have heels?"

"Am I living up to 'the authentic self' that I preach to my mentees when they ask how I'm so confident in a room where no one looks like me?"

"Why do I feel the need right now to change into the 'uniform of power' when I know I've busted my butt to get here, clothes-agnostic?"

"What's the worst that can happen?"

The *truth* is that I *trusted* all the hard work and preparation that led me to this moment. I was more than good enough as I was.

I ditched the heels, rocked the Js, and crushed the interview. What a journey to get to this moment!

I had been the pre-teen with thunder thighs who hated shopping for jeans, the student who was told she wasn't good enough by her teacher, and the executive who was struggling to fully live in her truth.

I made this decision for her.

When I shared this story in a post on LinkedIn shortly after the event, I received confirmation that all the struggles to get here were worth it. The post was so well received and met with unbelievable support from others who had felt the same at some point in their careers. They appreciated the level of authenticity that met this moment.

I was buoyed by the fact that no matter the path forward, I had the confidence I needed to step into any room as myself. No more hiding. No more playing small.

I knew my value.

LET'S RUN IT BACK:
KNOW YOURSELF TO KNOW YOUR WORTH

Too often, societal influence determines who we are to the world. I knew if I gave in to that influence, then I wouldn't be truly comfortable with the real me. I had to do the work,and I encourage you to do the same.

1. Define who you are before someone else does it for you. This will be your "center." The place for you to always come back to when doubt, fear, and trolls creep in.

2. Sit in and appreciate what makes you unique. There is no one like you, which means there is no one who can leverage what is unique to you and only you. Own it.

3. Your authentic self is good enough. When the time comes for you to tap into that, do it. Don't play small or shrink for anyone.

CHEAT CODE 2:
FIND YOUR PEOPLE

After years of fighting my battles alone, I leaned in to receive.

I discovered a circle of friends, family, and colleagues who nurtured and supported every one of my seemingly unimaginable dreams. They also corrected and challenged me from a place of love. When my confidence waned, they also reminded me who the hell I am.

In the second cheat code, you'll learn how and why I did the hardest thing for me to do: ask for help and then accept it. Opening up and showing vulnerability were two things I considered to be weaknesses. As a woman in business, I was taught that I should never show emotions, good or bad. Being seen as emotional as a leader was the kiss of death. However, the pressure became too great as I advanced.

Throughout my trials and successes, I saw my village being stitched together as I was enveloped with support and stewardship, but most importantly with love.

People come into your life for a reason, a season or a lifetime.

—JAY SHETTY

CHAPTER 5:

SAY YES FIRST

I am a loner but an ambivert. I am introverted at the core but extroverted to pay the bills. It still blows my mind that I chose a career where service and hospitality are the foundation.

I grew up in a relatively small family unit as I wasn't that close to members of my extended family. I am five years older than my sister, so we had separate lives growing up—she was entering middle school as I was ending my high school years. Our parents were "over-the-top supportive." Whatever we wanted to do, they said "Yes." I've already touched on my gymnastics career, but between me and my sister, we wanted to try it all: saxophone, trumpet, French horn, drums, karate, basketball, soccer, softball. It didn't matter because their answer was always "Yes." Looking back to this time, I think this was how I developed the "I can do anything I set my mind to" philosophy. Possibility surrounded us.

Outside my family, trust was earned, so I was and still am a private person. I also grew up in the generation of "don't share too much and keep your business within the family." I didn't have a circle of friends doing the traditional tween and teen stuff. Sure, I would go to an occasional sleepover or birthday party, but it was all surface-level.

I was more of a one-best-friend kind of girl.

My philosophy was to push all my emotions down. So as I graduated from college and began "adulting," I was again left with mostly surface-level relationships. When I was dreaming my big dreams and thinking about a job in sports, I didn't really tell anyone. I had planned this life as a future optometrist, with everyone rooting me on. Meanwhile, deep down, I knew I wanted to do something else. The back and forth in my mind and having to deal with the emotions of letting people down was stressful. It was lonely. And I wasn't in the business of disappointing people.

I always wondered what that time in my life could have been like had I allowed people in.

Once I made the painful, yet rewarding, decision to pursue sports and forego the life I had planned as an optometrist, I knew I didn't want to repeat the same mistake. I couldn't do it alone.

The sports industry is small and niche. When I got in, I looked around and didn't see many people who looked like me. I didn't see how they could empathize with the day-to-day grind of code-switching or presenting yourself as someone who should be taken seriously. At first, I didn't see how it was possible to form a real friendship and let people in. I thought, "How could these people possibly relate to the joys and pains of working in corporate America as a black woman?"

The journey was slow and methodical.

My first job at the NHL's Florida Panthers was tough. There were a few black employees, but one in particular welcomed me to South Florida with open arms—Chimere Henfield. She was the first one to introduce me to industry politics and how best to navigate them. She also invited me to her church, and I'm glad I said *yes*. It helped me form a community that would be a support for me. This was my first time living outside of Alabama, so it was nice to have a place to go where I felt familiarity. I grew up in the church, so it felt like home to me even with my internal struggle of being gay, but not "out."

Chimere was "my people."

When I took the job at the Pittsburgh Pirates and looked around at my peers on the sales leadership team, I went back into protection mode. They were all white—four out of the five were white males. I thought, "Yeah, no. I can't trust these people." All of them were from the Midwest. As a southerner, I lumped them into the same type of people I grew up with in Alabama—close-minded, with little exposure to black people in their circles.

I'm glad I was wrong.

My teammate, Justin—whose wife outed me—became one of my closest friends despite not being able to fully relate to what I was experiencing. We shared our hopes and fears, along with those unimaginable dreams we could see in the distance. To him, I wasn't a collection of checked boxes. I was a "badass" who could ascend the ranks, not because I was black, or a woman, but because I was great at what I did. He was the first to speak out loud about the value I added just by being in the room.

I had another colleague, Travis, who oversaw another sales department. He and I hit it off over the love of our dogs and running. As I got to know him, I realized that he, too, was as ambitious and entrepreneurially-minded as I was. I tried not to dwell on the fact that his path and exposure as a white male would be drastically different from mine. Instead, I focused on how good a friend he was when I spoke about how I wanted to be a "boss" in this industry. His advice came from a place of support, often with replies of "how can I help?"

I said *yes* to opening myself up and welcoming support from others who didn't look like me. Travis and Justin were "my people."

Throughout the early years in sales leadership, I had several bosses and colleagues who cheered me on both up close and from afar. They believed in me.

One was Chris Zaber, my boss at the Pirates, who told me I could lead a new department. I lacked confidence in myself and the tools I had in my toolbelt at the time, but he thought otherwise.

Another was Chris's boss, Lou DePaoli, who helped me chart my path to the league office because he once had the role I was hoping to get.

Another was Brendan Donohue, my boss at the NBA league office, who helped coach me through my first-ever presentation in front of over three hundred people.

They were all white males, and I said *yes* to their help. They were also "my people."

Before all these relationships, I'd limited myself to only opening up to people who could be my "friends." My aperture was too narrow because I thought I could only trust and accept people who could truly understand me in every way.

I was wrong—again.

Through these relationships, my confidence grew. I became more comfortable owning my seat at the table. On the surface, it could look like that comfort came from having white males validate me. Trust me, this was an internal battle I often had with myself. As a self-described loner, why was I only connecting with white males who had no idea what I was really going through? Why were *they* my people? They didn't know what it was like to be in the closet, but have to fight to show up with a smile on my face and produce at work. They didn't have people in their ear telling them to keep their locs short so they could maintain some sense of "executive presence" to their white colleagues. They didn't have to be two different people: by day juggling the respectability factor in their professional world and by night being reintroduced to their full selves to catch their breath. It didn't connect at first. Then it clicked.

These were my people because there is no way I would have made it through my first seven years in sports without them. As hard as it is was for me to admit at the time, I needed them. I was still learning who I was. Their support buoyed me as I was furiously treading to stay afloat while questioning every move. Coming to terms with that was when I put my pride aside. Being in position to say "Yes, I need help" was a big step outside my comfort zone. But it was one I'm glad I took.

However, I knew for me to take the leap from a mid-level executive to a senior-level executive, I had to be more intentional with whom I surrounded myself. As a rising executive, the challenges I faced began to crystalize. I needed a nurturing support circle that understood me in a way that others had not to this point. I began to ask myself, "Who will help me when doubt and fear creep in? As the inevitable imposter syndrome rears its ugly head, who do I need on speed dial to bring me back to center?"

During my first four years at the NBA league office, my career was rapidly growing. I started as a director, and I was promoted two times within those four years. I was still in "prove-them-right" mode. I had formed some friendships, but I was so focused on proving that the gamble they took on me was worth it. My time there was a stepping stone, so I had little time to waste on my journey to the next step—the C-suite for a sports team. The department I worked in, team marketing and business operations (TMBO), was known for churning out talent that could be placed at a team for immediate impact. During my tenure, I was laser focused on learning as much about sports business operations as possible, so I could be counted in that number. I was well on my way.

However, something was missing and a familiar feeling was creeping in. I'd reverted back to the teenager and young adult who felt like she didn't need anyone. My head was down and focused on the destination, much like it was when I decided to dump optometry school and try sports. I began to feel alone.

Out of the comfort zone I go. I prayed for a willingness to open up and for the right person to show themselves to me.

In TMBO, there was one other black woman, Liliahn, who had ascended the ranks and was in the role I was trying to get to. She must have sensed me floating with no tether. It probably wasn't hard though. I wasn't big on small talk or making connections. She took me under her wing, not just professionally, but personally. She opened the doors to meeting other black women within the company. I was embarrassed to admit that I didn't even know these women existed. They shared some of the same fears, challenges, and doubts. But we also celebrated each other's successes. We built each other up in a world that would often beat us down. From the moment I met these women, I was at home. I wasn't alone. I knew I would forever have a place to go to be myself—fully.

I said *yes* to vulnerability, and my prayer was answered. They were "my people."

Fortunately, my support circle has widened over time. By the time I made it to TMBO, my identity and worth were tied to what I did for a living. I was the girl who worked in sports. The one who could get you tickets to any sporting event or concert. The one who had the cool job.

Once I realized I needed to be more than just my job, I sought out relationships with people who could not care less about what I did for a living. I wanted them to care about me for me, job or no job. So I turned to my family. I used to avoid sharing "work stuff" with my family. I would say to myself,

"What can they offer? They already think I work too much, and they don't know the sports industry."

I couldn't have been more wrong—again.

When I opened up to April, my mom, and my sister, I was surprised at the perspective they offered. I've cried, complained, and written off my career many times. I needed to have people in my corner who knew and understood me regardless of my career or what they could get from me. It took me a while to understand and embrace that. The support and grace shown to me by people who have no idea what I do and, quite frankly, don't care what I do has been invaluable. I'm beyond grateful.

Opening myself up to accept this help has not only made me a better leader, but also a better human. I needed to say *yes* to all these relationships. I needed to invite these people into my journey. Conversely, they needed to say *yes* to accepting the respective roles they played in my life.

In short, these are "my people." They are the people who remind me who the hell I am.

CHAPTER 6:

SAVE ME FROM MYSELF

———

I used to be a type A-plus personality. The kind of type A who craved perfection and lived in competition, sometimes even with myself. I'm not proud of this, but I used to call second-place finishers first losers. I recall someone asking me if I loved to win more than I hated to lose. I only had one right answer: I despised losing. Winning was an expectation. It was a mindset. I saw it like I saw breathing or blinking. Losing would literally take my breath away. I may or may not have thrown a full-blown temper tantrum when I got beat at The Game of LIFE board game. I was eight. It was bad.

I'm now a solid reformed A-minus. I'm still competitive, but winning isn't *as* important as it used to be. I'm more interested in the lessons learned when I don't succeed, hence the minus. But, there's still an A there because I have my father's work ethic and my mother's "stick-to-it-iveness."

My father, William, is a twin and the baby of nine siblings. His mother died when he was seven, and his father died when he was eleven. Growing up in poverty, simple things that meant survival were hard to come by. We never talked about it, but I believe his hard work was born out of a goal to break the generational cycle of poverty. He also sacrificed his own education to help his twin brother, a high school basketball star, attend college. My dad dropped out of community college and took a full-time job to support my uncle and his dream. He settled in at McDonald's, starting at the very bottom flipping hamburgers. When I was born, he was a manager of one location. Over time, I watched him put in the work and rise up to a regional manager overseeing multiple locations.

A man of few words and a million-dollar smile, he didn't talk to me about working hard. Instead, he showed me how it looked to be excellent in everything. I marveled at the way he spray starched his uniform each morning. There had to be a crease in the pants. A wrinkled uniform was unacceptable. Again, he never said, "Raven, iron your clothes," but I was watching. I never left the house with wrinkles. To this day, I iron my hoodies and sweatpants—weird, I know.

His employees respected him and some revered him. But they also had a healthy dose of fear. Not because he was a terrible boss, but because mediocrity was unacceptable. He demanded excellence.

I noticed the pride he took in his work. And he was good at it. I honestly noticed everything he did. He was meticulous and obsessive. And he worked a lot. But it drew me even closer to him. I associated pride with work; I also associated work with money.

So while I couldn't wait to start working, I really couldn't wait to start earning my own money. I hated asking my parents for things. For some reason, I was under the assumption that because I was a good kid with great grades, I should just get what I asked for, but that didn't fly in my house. When the moment came for me to earn some money, I jumped at it.

One summer, I went to visit my dad at McDonald's. I always wanted to hang out there. It was the summer between sixth and seventh grade. Kids were coming into their own with fashion: Guess Jeans, Duck Head shorts, and sneakers separated the "cool" from the "lame." I'll let you guess which bucket I fell into. My parents were not going to keep up with the Jones's, which meant the Jones's kids were irrelevant to them. I had to find a way to make some money!

As I was visiting with my dad, a birthday party was taking place in the new playground, or the PlayPlace as it was called. I noticed the cast of characters entertaining the kids: Ronald McDonald, Grimace, and Birdie the Early Bird. But there was one character missing—Hamburglar. He was the thieving character wearing horizontal stripes and a mask as if he was about to, well, participate in a burglary. My inquisitive eleven-year-old brain started spinning. Where was he? Why did they choose those three for this party? From what I could remember, Hamburglar was pretty short, so he wouldn't be as scary to the kids as a weird bird girl or a giant purple blob. And then it hit me.

"Dad, where is Hamburglar?" I asked.

"I don't know," he replied.

"Does he ever show up to the parties or is it just those three? How long are the birthday parties? Who is in the costumes? Are they McDonald's employees?" I badgered.

"Raven, I don't know. They're not employees. They're people we hire to put on the costumes. Why are you asking so many questions? Do you want to have your birthday party here?" he replied with an annoyed tone.

"Of course not!" I scoffed as any mature eleven-year-old would at the insinuation that a McDonald's birthday party was suitable for an almost-teenager.

"Well, what then?" he replied.

"Do you have a Hamburglar costume?" I asked.

It was almost as if something clicked for him as it was clicking for me. He smiled and said, "Yes."

He walked me back to the supply closet, opened the door, and took me to back to the far corner. This was where stuff went to die. The boxes were moldy and dusty. One was marked "Costumes." He dug through it and pulled out the Hamburglar hat. I smiled. Soon, he had the rest of the costume in his hands. And it smelled awful.

I didn't care. I saw opportunity. My dad saw initiative. We sealed the deal.

At eleven, I secured my first ever job as Hamburglar for the birthday parties at McDonalds. Fifty dollars for one party, or two hours of work. Some days, we had multiple parties. I approached this job as if I was auditioning for it every week. Because I was. My dad made it clear that I had to earn it. There were no handouts for the boss's kid. I wanted to be the best damn Hamburglar in Mickey D's birthday party history. I sought his feedback after every gig. I did fourteen birthday parties that summer and bought my first pair of Duck Head shorts.

In the '90s, employment at fast-food restaurants was the go-to for teenagers looking for part-time work, especially in a small town like Tuscaloosa, Alabama. This meant my dad was the boss to many of my and my sister's high-school classmates. All we ever heard from them was that he required perfection because he knew many of them would need to be better than average to excel. He took a personal interest in his employees, particularly those who came from a similar background as his. He wanted the best for them so they would want the best for themselves. When he passed away in 2019, the condolences and Facebook messages poured in. I heard stories about how his work ethic made a lasting impression on them. They went on and on about the impact he had on the adults they would become. He rarely explained the lessons as he was teaching them, but we always knew class was in session.

I miss him.

My mother, Dephrosia, on the other hand, was the epitome of the southern saying, "You catch more flies with honey than you do vinegar." The middle child of seven, she honed her charm and grit growing up in the church. Her father was an Apostolic Pentecostal preacher, but I never knew him. Her mother, Robbie, was the only grandparent I've ever known. She embodied the "strength of a black woman." She raised seven children with no high school diploma and a lot of prayer. After high school, my mom set out to become a nurse and attended Mississippi Valley State University, a historically black college in Itta Bena, Mississippi. The marching band was her calling—clarinet to be specific. Unfortunately, her college tenure was shortened due to a lack of financial support. She moved back to Tuscaloosa and in with her mom. Upon her arrival back home, she got a job at McDonalds.

She met a charming young man, who was assistant manager at the time. He was a man of few words with a million-dollar smile. A short time later, she gave birth to me. Realizing that the wage at McDonald's was unsustainable to care for a newborn, she made a change. Ever the independent woman, she wanted to be able to take care of me with or without my dad. They did eventually get married, but she still landed a full-time job at a local oil refinery.

It wasn't until retiring that she shared the endless stories of racism and sexism she faced in her forty-two years at the refinery. It was eye-opening. She had been passed over for promotions several times and was labeled "a troublemaker" as she attempted to fight for what she earned. Oftentimes, she would train people—white men—who would eventually become her bosses.

I knew it wasn't easy, but I had no idea what she went through. All I knew was that she was a present mother. She was at every single PTA meeting, and she was the president of the Booster Club of my high school basketball team. She

was always there. I never knew she dealt with Equal Employment Opportunity Commission (EEOC) complaints that
were ignored. I didn't think it was possible for me to love or
respect her any more than I already did.

As I was growing up, I never once heard her complain,
and she was always there when I needed her—always. It was
devastating to hear the stories of what she had to endure
at her job during that time. During her career, she pushed
through unbelievable and heartbreaking experiences. She
should write her own book to detail how a black woman
survived through those trying times. Too often, black women
have to be the "strong" one and soldier through despite what
the outside world is doing to try to break them. I know she
did it for our family, but she also did it to prove something
to herself. They were not going to break her. They were not
going to win.

I'm a good blend of the two of them. I won't say the perfect
blend though.

The inheritance of my dad's work ethic and pursuit of perfection, along with my mom's "push through and be strong
attitude" has not always served me well. I drowned myself in
my work and agonized over every single detail in my career.
It has cost me sleep, friendships, progeny, and several relationships. I'm not saying one should not work hard and make
sacrifices. All-nighters and late emails are required at times.
It just can't be every night. I was a workaholic who mistook
being busy and sending 2 a.m. emails as being productive.

When COVID-19 shut the world down on March 12, 2020,
my wife and I had to leave our home in Brooklyn. April is
immunocompromised, having received a double-lung trans-
parent in 2004. We didn't know much about the virus, other
than it was airborne and affected the lungs. We couldn't risk
her health with the cramped quarters and shared spaces that
were a staple in New York City. So, we escaped to Jacksonville,

Florida, to ride the pandemic out with my mother and father in-law. They were retired, so we could safely hunker down knowing they weren't being exposed to the virus daily. Days turned into weeks and weeks turned into eight months in total. We never lived in Brooklyn again.

During this time, I was at the NBA league office working for TMBO. I went from being on the road every week, in and out of airports and hotels, to a standstill working from home. In August of 2020, the stresses had ratcheted up with preparation for the 2020–21 NBA regular season rapidly approaching. I worked nonstop, answered emails during family dinner and movie nights, and paused morning workouts to answer phone calls. Layoffs were occurring at the league office, and I didn't want to be a casualty. I had to prove they needed me—but this was nothing new. I've always had to work twice as hard to get half as far. No time for down time. To me, this was business as usual.

My septuagenarian father-in-law, on the other hand, did not understand. I call him Pops.

On days where the stresses were just too much, I'd go outside to work by the pool. One day, Pops came out to join me. When he sat down, he had a look of disappointment on his face. He noticed the laptop in my lap.

"Good gosh, girl. Why are you working so much? You're going to look up and miss everything. Do you have a deadline or something?" Pops asked in his caring and soothing southern tone.

"Not particularly, I just have to get something done before dinner. I promise it won't take long," I replied, hoping he would understand.

"So, nothing's due right at this moment?" he asked in a confused tone.

"Um, no. It would just make me feel better if I got it done before I shut it down tonight," I said with annoyance.

"Well, when is shut down? I've never seen you 'shut it down.' You work all the time, even on weekends," he sarcastically replied.

"Yeah, I guess you're right," I replied.

He got up from the swing and went back inside. I rationalized in my head that he just didn't get it. In his day, they didn't have email, and there was no need to be "on" twenty-four-seven. They barely had phones. They had more job security. He was a white man who had retired with a pension. How could he understand the pressures I have on me?

I said this to myself to justify my maniacal approach to working ungodly hours. Yes, it is true that there is an unbearable pressure on me to perform as a black woman. But in this moment, why couldn't I just sit with Pops and enjoy the sway of the porch swing on that particular summer evening? Why did I feel like I needed to be "on"? He was right. I could look up and miss the most important moments. Moments that would never happen again.

I closed my laptop and leaned back on the swing. I shut my eyes, inhaled, then exhaled slowly. When I opened my eyes, the wind was blowing, and the trees were swaying back and forth. It occurred to me that I'd never watched trees sway—ever. In that moment, tears began to fill my eyes. Feeling the breeze and watching each tree pass the wind along to the next. *This* must have been what being present felt like. This was the slowing down Mom would tell me about as I rushed her off the phone to get to my next work call. This was what my father-in-law wanted to do with me. Sit and swing while watching the trees sway.

Being present was important. Knowing how to control what I could control was important. Not just for me, but for the people who matter most to me.

As much as I needed people to support my dreams and remind me who the hell I am, I also needed them to save me from myself. I need them to remind me to really shut down when I go on vacation. I need to be told I am good enough even if I don't feel like it. I need that safe space to be imperfect with no pressure. I don't always need to be "on." Sometimes "no" is the right response.

Through all of this, I realized I needed to be told to stop, breathe, and reflect as much as I needed affirmation.

CHAPTER 7:

SURROUNDED BY CHALLENGERS

———

Early in my career, I ran in circles exclusively within the sports industry. Most of my closest associates were peers at other teams at the same level in their careers as me. In the Big Four sports leagues—NBA, NFL, NHL, and MLB—there are a total of 124 teams and most have the same staffing structure. This means for most positions, there are only 124 other people in that role, but sometimes less. It's a very small and incestuous world. Everyone knows everyone, which can be a positive when you need someone to vouch for you as you grow within the ranks. When I left the Florida Panthers to pursue a stretch role at the Pittsburgh Pirates, the hiring manager called my boss at the Panthers who gave me a glowing recommendation. I was a beneficiary of that small incestuous world, particularly at the mid-managerial level.

Conversely, when it came to learning and sourcing the tools to grow into the C-suite and beyond, my world was small. I didn't branch outside my small circle. I didn't build connections that offered differing perspectives. I had people around me who thought just like me. After all, they were at the same level. We were all very comfortable.

"Comfortable" scares me. I felt uneasy. In my mind, I wasn't growing or learning. So how did I open myself up to reach for the uncomfortable?

I took baby steps.

When I went to the NBA league office in 2015, my experience was primarily in the sales and marketing space. By its nature of consultation, TMBO provided me with exposure to other areas of the business. However, many of the people in TMBO had similar backgrounds as me. So, while I was being stretched and challenged in my role, I wasn't necessarily broadening my circle of peers. I thought a good first step would be to build a relationship with someone in another department.

I didn't force it, but I was intentional. I was looking for something specific. Someone who I could learn from, but also someone who I could see myself having a glass of wine with after work. I was asking a lot, but the introvert in me was searching for commonality in the connection.

It didn't happen overnight.

In 2018, I was on a committee working on an NBA league-led Women's Forum designed to empower and inspire women at our teams. This committee consisted of strongly opinionated women. I was envious and intimidated at the same time. They spoke so eloquently and succinctly on their points—it was something to behold and learn from. In scenarios like this, I tended to shy away from speaking up unless I knew exactly what I wanted to say. I never wanted to speak just to speak. I wanted my words to mean something. I was always searching for the proverbial "head nod" of acceptance.

During one of our meetings, a woman gave a thoughtful and insightful recommendation that not only got the "head nod," but an immediate approval. Morgan Cato worked in a different department—basketball operations. She was not the chair of the committee, but when she spoke, she commanded the room and people listened. Poise and confidence radiated from her. I wanted to be like her.

Only one thing was holding me back—stereotypes, or as a better term, tropes.

I never wanted to be the black woman people viewed as aggressive, loud, or angry. Navigating primarily white spaces, I knew that would be my fate if ever I spoke up in a way that wasn't measured and methodical. I literally thought about every single inflection, eye movement, neck position, and hand gesture when I spoke in those rooms—which was exhausting.

Morgan singlehandedly dismantled every trope that black women drag into boardrooms. Her confidence stood above everything else.

During our next committee meeting, I gathered up the courage to tell her how much her presence meant to me. Specifically, how she carried herself so boldly and with little hesitation or trepidation. Her climb uphill was even more steep than mine. She was charting a path no other woman had reached in basketball operations. I saw *some* women at the CEO level on the business side of sports, so I knew it could be done.

In our conversations, she shared that she didn't want to get to the top unless she could be herself doing it, Brooklyn swagger and all. When she revealed that her confidence came from overpreparing, something clicked. It came from knowing that whatever anyone threw her way, she would be ready. Until that moment, I had been doubting myself and not trusting in my own preparation. But I didn't need to overthink—because the work had already been done. Overpreparation was the tool I didn't know I needed. She helped me find my voice.

Morgan eventually rose to the ranks of assistant general manager and vice president of basketball operations for the

Phoenix Suns, which made her the first woman of color to hold that position in the NBA.

The first baby step outside my comfort zone was a success. I had now started down the path of surrounding myself with people who challenged me for the better.

On to the next step.

My role at the league office brought an opportunity to learn and develop skills I didn't know I needed. I was traveling every week, consulting on business practices at six different NBA franchises. Relationship-building was at the core of the strategic partnerships being formed. I was in a groove. I loved it.

And then, the world stopped on March 12, 2020.

Coronavirus was a "thing" I heard about on the nightly news. It had not reached home yet, but that all changed on March 11, 2020. Rudy Gobert, the center for the Utah Jazz, tested positive, causing their game against the Oklahoma City Thunder to be canceled. By sheer coincidence, I had just returned to Brooklyn from Salt Lake City six days earlier. The Utah Jazz was one of the teams in my consultation portfolio.

On March 12, my world, and the world of my colleagues, at the league office stopped and then kicked into high gear all at once. We were no longer able to travel after living life on the road. Our day-to-day routines radically changed. We went into planning mode to help our teams prepare to get back on the court safely when all this was over. Little did we know, "over" was a misnomer.

Uncertainty and stress filled the subsequent months. The 2019–20 NBA season was cut short in March, but it resumed with one of the most impressive feats I've seen in sports: the Bubble in Orlando. Through rigorous testing, tight security protocols, and limited contact from the outside world, players, coaches, and staff descended upon Disney in July to finish what they started. The NBA was back.

By then, I had relocated to Jacksonville with my in-laws and was searching for an opportunity to stretch myself. I was afraid if I didn't take on more or use this opportunity to acquire new skills, then I would get too comfortable. I didn't want to just wait to get back on the road and back to what I was doing before everything shut down.

Time to get uncomfortable.

Several projects were coming down the pipeline. One was the least sexy of them all—a cross-departmental project to create arena protocols for the safe return of basketball at our team's arenas. We were coming off the Bubble in Orlando where we had some control. But we were still in a pandemic heading into the 2020–21 season. We needed protocols for *everything*: path of travel for players and fans, socially-distanced seating configurations, cleaning, sanitation, you name it. All of which I had no experience in.

I sought advice from my boss, Matt. I wanted to know: Was this project a good use of my time? Will I be taken away from another opportunity to hone skills that would be more beneficial—a.k.a. more sexy? After assuring me it would be a good project to take on, I begrudgingly raised my hand. If for nothing else, I would expand my network within the league and learn more about how other departments serve our franchises.

The project did that and more.

When the league creates new rules or guidelines that affect the teams, we seek the advisement of the presidents at the teams—captains, so to speak. This project was no different. Our captain was Peter Feigin, president of the Milwaukee Bucks.

The project ran from April through September of 2020. This meant several calls a month with our working group and Peter. Over time, he and I made a connection. He was a gregarious and innovative leader; he didn't take himself too seriously. From afar, I admired what he and his team had built in Milwaukee.

In the Bubble in Orlando, the Bucks grabbed my attention in another way. They took a stand to protest the shooting of Jacob Blake in Kenosha, Wisconsin, choosing not to play their game against the Orlando Magic. It was the first domino to fall as MLB, the WNBA, and MLS followed suit with protests of their own.

Out of the blue, in September of 2020, Peter reached out to me to discuss a role he had been noodling on for some time. He needed a number two—someone to oversee the day-to-day operations of the business. There was also an opportunity that this person could be the heir to the presidency. Of course, I was intrigued. But was I ready? I was thriving and learning in my position at the league, but there was something pulling me to Milwaukee, the city, the role. It just felt right.

I sought advice from two of my closest confidants, Stacy and Pam. They both reminded me that I specifically came to the league for an opportunity like this. Stacy was a friend from TMBO, and she was someone whose opinion I valued. She outlined all the tools and knowledge I collected along the way that would serve me well as I transitioned to an executive at the team level. Pam, a C-level executive and a black woman who knew what the road behind and the road ahead looked like for me, offered to help me with salary negotiations once I got to that nerve-racking part of the process. Their ultimate advice was that I was more than ready, and I should pursue it wholeheartedly.

The conversation with Peter began in September. By December, I was agreeing to an offer to become the executive vice president of business operations for the Milwaukee Bucks.

The people who joined me along my path to the Bucks challenged me in several ways: Matt supported my desire to acquire new skills despite them not being directly applicable to my "day job." Stacy's advice set the stage for me to deliver clear and concise reasons to Peter and his team on why I was ready to take this leap. Once I received the offer, Pam led me down the path of "owning and confidently requesting" a salary that was commensurate with my experience. They were my dream team of challengers.

Saying yes to opportunities that stretched me both mentally and physically, explaining my value to others, and knowing my worth were the next set of tools I added to my toolbelt. They served me well as I navigated unknown and uncomfortable spaces.

On to the next step.

Within a few months of taking the job with the Bucks, I started receiving calls from headhunters, or recruiters as they are more commonly called these days. In my mind, I had not done nearly enough to warrant a conversation for a president or CEO role. I didn't learn this until later, but it wasn't uncommon for people to leave jobs after only a few months to jump at a higher title. That didn't make sense to me. Although the calls were intriguing, I couldn't leave in good faith before I put my mark on the role. I couldn't leave before I could honestly say I left the organization better than I found it.

I was happy in my position. I was making an impact. Although there was no wavering or doubt in my mind that the destination was the presidency or CEO job at a team in one of the core four sports leagues—NBA, NFL, NHL, or MLB—the timing wasn't right. I made my goal clear to the recruiters, so they knew what I needed to accomplish and where I ultimately wanted to be when I felt my work was done in my current role as EVP.

There was a lull of about a year and a half.

Then the calls began again. I had been executive vice president for almost two years. There were a few COO roles and even fewer president jobs being presented from the recruiters. I took a step back and zoomed out to take a thirty-thousand-foot view of the roles being pitched to me, but they were not in the core four leagues. Why was that? I specifically stated my goals of being in the core four sports leagues. I noticed a theme. I began to think this was going to be as high as I was going to be able to go in sports. The only leagues willing to "take a gamble on me" were ones that weren't in the core four.

Until this point, I had not discussed any of the recruiter conversations with anyone in my circle. But I needed to talk to someone. I decided to share these conversations with Malcolm, a black executive in the C-suite at another team and a close friend. When I shared with him, I learned his own experience had been almost identical. At one point, he had received the same calls I was getting.

I noticed a pattern.

Malcolm's goal was the same as mine: president or CEO at the highest level of professional sports. He told the recruiters the same thing. He was already at the number two spot at his team and was ready to make the leap. He was ready to run the show. However, the difference between us was that he trained recruiters not to approach him with roles that didn't fit his goals. My mistake was trying to handle it with my "southern politeness." I had to be kind and take the call to hear them out, but I silently seethed because I had to remind them I wasn't interested in anything other than the NHL, NFL, MLB, or NBA.

This was not Malcolm's approach. He had been adamant that if they called or emailed him about anything other than core four opportunities, his only response would be "I'm happy to check my network to see who may be a good fit." I read between the lines. He was saying, "I'm not settling for what you think is the next step for me. I will not be deterred because I know I've done the work to be considered for a president or CEO role at a core four sports team. I know I can take that on with the same level of excellence as I've done with everything."

Malcolm taught me that I should never settle. He also taught me to never take it personally. Focus on the goal. He convinced me that it's not the recruiter's job to believe in me. That's my job. They're not focused on the impact I can make at my next stop when I run the show. Their job is to cast a wide enough net with the hopes of someone being "the one" for their role. I had let them convince me I was only good enough to be considered for lesser roles. I had not been strong enough in my conviction to tell them I'm not settling for what they say I'm worthy of or ready for.

After this lesson, my new mantra became "don't settle."

I know what I want for myself. I know what I'm ready for. Malcolm reminded me of that and challenged me to see my value.

On to the next step, only bigger and bolder.

I continue to be in awe of what a title like executive vice president can do to open doors, particularly working in the sports industry with its "cool factor." I intentionally sought out networking circles that would not only expose me to minorities at the executive level outside sports, but also BIPOC start-up founders and private equity firm owners.

Paris Wallace grew up in Northern California to humble beginnings. His mother was disabled and raised him and his brother on her own. Her life's work was ensuring they had every single advantage she could afford them, with education at the core. Despite being dyslexic and having severe ADHD, Paris attended the best of the best private schools beginning at three years old, all the way through Amherst for his undergraduate degree and Harvard Business School for his graduate degree. He knew his path was entrepreneurship, having started his first company in his dorm room at Amherst. He has since gone on to own several businesses, most notably, Ovia Health, a leading digital health platform for women and families.

Paris came into my life through a series of encounters that never would have happened if I had not set out to think beyond the sports industry and expand my network. After exiting Ovia, he looked for his next challenge. A serial entrepreneur, his love of cycling birthed a start-up Criterium racing (Crit) league called the National Cycling League (NCL). Crit is a mass start, multi-lap event contested on a closed course where laps are typically a mile or less and include four to six corners. As an avid sports fan, it's no surprise I fell in love with Crit the moment I saw it. It's like Formula One meets Tour de France.

NCL's goal was to disrupt the traditional league format. It was already bucking trends by being the only minority-owned league and paying both men and women cyclists the same salary—equity and inclusion right out of the gate. They were looking for a president to build, lead, and grow the league, which led Paris to me.

We discussed the presidency. He was a visionary, and the opportunity to work alongside a serial entrepreneur with a clear vision was beyond intriguing. In our brief conversation, I learned more about capitalization tables, sustainable growth, and disruption than in all my previous seventeen years in the sports industry. Ultimately, the timing wasn't right as I was still bullish on what we could accomplish at the Bucks. But despite turning down the opportunity, I was still challenged.

My mind began to race. I was thinking of all the possibilities I could have if I took my limits off. What would happen if I invested as much in myself as I do making money for others? Ambition grabbed a hold of me.

I originally told myself that president or CEO was the destination. I assumed that was the end of the journey. But after my conversation with Paris, I wanted a seat at a different table—my table. All this time, I thought the best I could do to "represent" possibility was to be seen doing what few others, if any, had done. I thought a black, queer woman ascending to the ranks of president or CEO for a sports team was the ultimate destination. But I needed exposure to the conversations that we're rarely privy to—the conversations where cap tables, equity, and ownership are the goals.

I no longer had limits to what I could see myself doing. I had Paris to thank for that.

When I look back at how I got to where I am today, it isn't only because everyone in my life cheered me on. It is also because I opened myself to people who would challenge me to think beyond my self-imposed limits and help me procure the tools necessary to secure what is possible.

I needed to surround myself with challengers. These were people like Morgan, Stacy, Pam, Peter, Malcolm, and Paris. People who push, educate, and inspire me beyond my comfort zone. Surrounding myself with these types of people challenge me to stop just existing and start thriving.

LET'S RUN IT BACK:
FIND YOUR PEOPLE

My support circle nurtured and buoyed my unimaginable dreams, but it also corrected me with love. I'm currently living in the dream I saw for myself twenty years ago, but I thought I had no real path of achieving it. When I left society's goal of being an optometrist, the unwavering support of my parents was the first sign that the people surrounding me would be there through my rise and fall—particularly the falls. My unrelenting commitment to excellence and the pursuit of perfection left me susceptible to ignoring the impact on the people in my life and, conversely, their impact on me.

1. When I think back to many of the mistakes early in my career, there is one theme that stands out: I went through them alone. You can't make it on your own with only your lessons to learn from. You will face obstacles, but they are a little easier to get through when you share them with someone and say "yes" to letting them in.

2. You need to be reminded that what you do for a living is not the only value you offer the world. Being "on" all the time us unsustainable, impractical, and unhealthy. It's okay to lean on your support circle as they envelope your imperfections and embrace your flaws.

3. Surround yourself with people who are different from you. People who have different backgrounds and education levels, but mostly people who challenge you and offer different perspectives. Diversity is equally as important for your support circle as it is for the boardroom.

CHEAT CODE 3:
PAUSE, REFLECT, AND REINVEST

The road has been tough. I almost left the sports industry. But instead, I paused to take a breath and refilled my cup with the pieces of joy I needed to find balance. I reflected to assess and celebrate what I had accomplished while adjusting the expectations of perfection I had for myself. Then I reinvested in the skills I needed to continue down the road at the highest possible level.

In this third cheat code, you'll learn how the race to the top almost broke me. I bought into it all—black excellence, black girl magic. I got caught up in what my achievements could mean for someone who looked like me or loved like me. I was so concerned with how failure could close the door for others in marginalized communities. It had to stop.

I began centering myself and focusing on what my needs were first. I gave myself grace and realized I couldn't continue to pour into others without pouring into me.

When you take care of yourself, you're a better person for others. When you feel good about yourself, you treat others better.

—SOLANGE KNOWLES

CHAPTER 8:

EMOTIONAL TAXATION

For most of my career, I categorized feelings of fear, doubt, judgment, and exhaustion as weaknesses. Specifically, weaknesses that I, as a black woman, couldn't afford to express. Our patriarchal and ableist society demanded I had to repress them. Despite being a classic "overthinker," I never allowed myself to sit in them for too long. If I did, they consumed me. They paralyzed me. In my mind, I couldn't possibly get to the top if I experienced them. I certainly couldn't express to anyone else that I was feeling them because I always had to be "on."

I had two definitions for "on."

On top of my job to be the best. I never wanted anyone to see me slip. I also had to be *on* guard twenty-four-seven. Did I ever say something that would characterize me as an angry black woman? Was my hair considered too ethnic? Should I work on my southern accent as not to be seen through the stereotypes of being slow or unintelligent? Was I exhibiting the executive presence that I hear so many talk about but never explain? I fell victim to the game of respectability defined by Merriam-Webster as "worthy of respect" or "decent or correct in character or behavior." I had a fear of being the stereotypical black woman who never made it to the C-suite because I was "difficult to work with" or intimidating. The fear was real.

I recall trying to prove I was "worthy of respect" in my first sports job at the Florida Panthers. Our CEO at the time was known for his intensity and 4 a.m. emails before his workouts. I, too, was an early riser and knew he worked out with his personal trainer in our company gym. Instead of working out at my apartment gym, I had the genius idea to take my 4:30 a.m. workouts to the company gym. Inside the genius idea was the hope that the CEO would notice me. After all,I was one of eleven on the entry-level sales team, and I had no connections in the industry. I was looking for an edge.Honestly, I had no clue what I would do if he said something to me or even what I was hoping to accomplish with this strategy. I hadn't thought that far ahead.

Morning after morning, I'd walk into the gym, head-phones on, and my workout would commence. Gym time was my time. I zoned out and focused on the sixty to seventy-five minutes ahead. This went on for weeks. Just me, him, and his trainer walking past each other in a sweat box as if the other didn't exist. He never acknowledged me.

What a waste of time.

Until one fateful day at an all-staff meeting.

At the end of the meeting, I stood with a few of my fellow sales reps when he walked by.

"Raven. How was the workout this morning?" he shouted as he made his way to the exit.

Stunned, I replied, "It was amazing. How was yours?"

"Great. See you tomorrow," he replied.

The entire interaction took, maybe, six seconds. The other sales reps were in shock and began to ask all kinds of questions. I had one question of my own: How did he know my name?

It turns out, he had asked my boss's boss about the "woman who was making him feel bad in the gym," in jest of course. My plan had worked. Or at least, in my mind, I hoped I could make someone see me as something other than the tropes that were laid upon black women. I was also somehow revered by my fellow sales reps because the CEO "knew my name." Looking back on it, this was the most ridiculous play for attention and respect. But these were the types of gymnastics and games I felt I had to play to get noticed.

This was when I knew I had to take on a second job: fighting stereotypes.

During my early days in management at the Pittsburgh Pirates, I was still developing my leadership style. I wanted to be stern, but approachable. I was so committed to my sales team's success that I would often sit out in the sales bullpen with them and coach on the spot. I wanted them to see me as a supportive leader.

One day, on my way to grab coffee, I walked by another sales team, waved, and said, "Good morning." This team consisted of entry-level salespeople right out of college, which was the first job for most of them. I noticed most mornings when I spoke to them, they barely acknowledged me. This morning was no different. Most people I knew in sales were outgoing and boisterous, so their lack of response surprised me. They were beyond quiet and were more like a deer in headlights. After enough encounters of awkwardness, I finally asked their boss, Travis, why his team was so shy. His answer shook me.

"They're intimidated by you. You should smile more."

What? How were they intimidated by me? I'm the one who speaks to them every single morning. I'm approachable. I'm nice. Hell, I'm southern! I know what hospitality and charm is. What was I doing that intimidated these kids? I saw them speak to all the other leaders, so they clearly could open their mouths to say hello to others. What was different about me?

There was only one black employee on the entry-level sales team. The others were white. The other sales leaders were white. I internalized their lack of response. It felt to me that they were more comfortable and saw the other leaders as more welcoming.

As the only black person and one of two women on the leadership team at the time, my biggest fear was playing out right in front of me. No matter what I did, how I dressed, or how I spoke, I was still the intimidating black woman who was unapproachable.

I went back to my office and closed the door. I felt myself getting angry. I knew I didn't have time to be angry. There was no time to sulk and question why these people felt this way about me. I had to collect myself.

Cue, "Dirt Off Your Shoulder" by Jay-Z.

Music was my way of zoning out. A form of meditation, so to speak, that accompanied the self-talk and affirmations I needed to get back on track.

"Continue to focus on the things you can control. These people don't know you. It is not your responsibility to change how people feel about you. You are worthy. You are enough."

I collected myself, walked out of the office, and headed to my next meeting.

Doubt and judgment are fear's best friends.

The price of doubt is daunting. As I've grown in my career, the amount of time I spend doubting and judging myself has lessened, but they both creeped in at the most inopportune times.

After I had my first call with Peter about the executive vice president role at the Milwaukee Bucks in the fall of 2020, there was a moment of extreme excitement. All the work to this point had paid off. I was finally getting a chance to speak to my accomplishments and how I could add value to an organization.

That was short-lived—the doubt quickly took over.

I had never led a team or business at this level.

I wouldn't have any credibility with an already established executive team.

I was probably just a diversity interview for Peter to add to his slate of interviews. He must have had this conversation because of the racial reckoning happening in our country right now.

As always, he would go with another, more established, white male and wouldn't seriously consider me for this role.

The negative thoughts I was telling myself were plentiful. I doubted myself so much that I didn't even tell my wife, April, about the job at first. I didn't want her to see my level of excitement because deep down I just knew this wasn't real. I was so angry and hard on myself. The self-talk that occurred was a conversation no one should have with oneself. No one was harder on me than me.

Why was I allowing my fears and doubts to creep into my psyche like this? The back and forth happening between my ears was exhausting. But there was no time to linger. I sat in my feelings just long enough to appreciate them. I collected myself and realized I had earned the right to continue my conversations with Peter and go into the process wholeheartedly. Ultimately, I knew I should be considered for this role. I wanted to silence the inner critic and prove to myself and others that I could do the job.

I thought that once I got in the groove of the job, my doubt and fears would subside. They did for a little while, but after a conversation with another woman in the industry, they came flooding back like a tidal wave.

A few months after taking the job at the Bucks, I was invited to speak on a panel at a conference. It was one of the first conferences back in person after things reopened "post COVID-19." It would be good to see people in person again after years of Zoom calls and virtual meetings. It was also great knowing that I would be able to connect with the small contingent of minority leaders at or near my level. With so few black women in leadership in my industry, we felt like were with family any time we saw each other at these events. It felt like home. It was a safe space to take a collective breath and gather ourselves before heading into a ballroom where few others looked like us.

At the social event, the night before the conference began, I met eyes with Amber, a black woman who was a senior executive from another team. We abandoned our separate conversations and made an immediate beeline toward each other. We talked as if we hadn't seen each other in years. There was a welcomed familiarity. She showed me photos of her kids and shared how things were going for her in her role. When she asked me how things were for me, the conversation took a turn I was not prepared for:

"How are things in Milwaukee? You know what, I don't even know why I'm asking. I don't have to ask how things are going for you!" Amber said with a sheepish smirk on her face.

"Why is that?" I asked nervously and defensively.

Amber replied, "Girl, you are everywhere. I see you on LinkedIn. I can't make it through my feed without seeing a shout out to you, an award you've received, a podcast you're on. You're doing everything."

"Hmm, yeah. It's not really my style, but I guess it comes with the job. I hate it. I just want to do the work. You know we have to work a hundred times harder than everyone else," I replied.

"I don't know about that. How long have you been on the job? I need your publicist. They have you out there as their face of diversity. They're clearly milking this hire for all it's worth. I'm happy for you. I have to go meet my colleagues inside," Amber said before hugging me and walking away.

I was speechless. All the fears and doubts came flooding in, and the safe space I thought I was in at this moment disappeared. Amber was someone I respected. But now, even she was saying I was simply a means to an end for diversity. My mind began to race. If she's feeling this way, others must as well. Maybe I don't belong here. Maybe I am just here because it makes the Milwaukee Bucks look good.

I've had similar conversations like this before, but there was a judgment in her tone. I didn't feel supported. I thought of all people, she would be able to empathize with my situation. We were family. It was painful to hear my "family" speak this way. I wasn't sure if she was judging me, the Bucks, the complex systems at play, or all of the above. Regardless, the judgment was paralyzing.

I left the event and went back to my hotel room. I needed to regroup and prepare for my panel the following day. I reminded myself that I had earned my spot as executive vice president. The hard work that I put in had paid off. Yes, I hated the spotlight that Amber judged me for, but someone needed to see me in this space. What I was doing was not about me or Amber, it was about what is possible when preparation meets opportunity. I was doing this for them.

Siri, play "Crown" by Jay-Z.

I woke up the next morning feeling refreshed and ready to crush the panel.

I spent countless hours agonizing over what to wear, how to speak, and how to wear my hair. All to fit an immeasurable and impossible narrative of how to achieve success and access to power. The emotional tax was a burden. The mental gymnastics that black women have to play just to get through the day is exhausting; constant microaggressions play out in the scenes of my professional life.

I hadn't stopped to examine the toll that doubt, fear, and judgment were taking on my life. I was on autopilot and moving past them as if they didn't exist, telling myself this was just part of being me in spaces not built for me. There would always be people who would assume I didn't earn the right to be here. I would just have to deal with it. But I wasn't dealing with it—I was ignoring the toll it was taking.

I wasn't sleeping. My love for wine turned into a need for a glass or three a night. I was taking out my frustration on my wife, causing strain on my relationship. In turn, I poured myself even more into work as I ignored the signs.

This was unsustainable. I knew if I didn't do something, my career and my marriage would be short-lived.

CHAPTER 9:

REFLECTION AND REST

———

The plane ride home from that conference was an inflection point.

Over those four hours, I reckoned with the realization that my emotional well-being was in a delicate state. The culmination of sleepless nights, the stress created by constantly navigating uncomfortable spaces not suited for me, the constant burying of the emotions I was experiencing, and the daily drinking had all finally caught up with me. I knew I couldn't sustain this existence. I needed to develop a better set of skills to not only survive but thrive in the second half of my career.

When I returned home, I sat down with April to do something I had never done before, at least not well: I talked about all my feelings. Not just the fluffy, surface-level feelings of "Oh, I'm tired" or "I'm stressed." I got deep for the first time. This was a *huge* step. Until this moment, I had never discussed the real impact my experiences had on me. Yes, I had people I could talk to and commiserate with about how a situation made me feel. But what happened with April was an unloading of years of stress, pain, and exhaustion.

I was beyond tired. The sobbing was uncontrollable.

On the surface, I was just getting in a groove. I loved my job in Milwaukee. The Bucks were coming off a championship season. Life was great. I should have been grateful, with no complaints at all. I was living the life I prayed and worked hard for. This should not have been happening.

Below the surface, however, I was broken. I had buried so many of my feelings. I rarely took days off, and when I did, I still obsessed about work and what was happening while I was away. I was endlessly checking and responding to emails, and thinking that what I did was so important the place would catch fire if I wasn't there. Weeklong vacations? No way. The first and only time I took a "vacation" longer than a few days was my honeymoon in 2017, eleven years after I started working in sports. I didn't take my laptop because I would have been divorced before I returned to the states. There was no such thing as "me time" or "self-care." I felt like I had to go, go, go to reach the levels of success I aspired to.

In my mind, I told myself the journey led to a destination. On that journey, I had to put in the work and sacrifice all things that didn't put me closer to that goal—to be a team president or CEO. Everything else be damned. But once I got there, I would be happy. I would take some time to rest. I would revel and relish in the accomplishments and finally put myself first. I would finally be satisfied.

But on that plane ride home from the conference, I knew that would never be true. I would never be satisfied. I remembered something my mom always told me.

"You can't pour from an empty cup. If you were no longer on this Earth, the people at work would mourn you, of course. But that place will keep going. You get one life, one chance. What are you doing with it?"

I couldn't count the number of times she said that to me prior to recalling this memory. She was giving me the gift of perspective, but I wasn't ready to receive it...until this moment when I couldn't control my tears. As morbid as it sounded, she was right.

My cup was empty. My soul was empty. I had nothing left to give.

I explained this to April as she consoled me and tried to empathize. She tried her best to help. But the only person who could help me was me. I had to approach this situation differently than I had any other because the stakes were higher. I had to make different decisions. My mental well-being was at stake. As I gathered myself, I decided in that moment to do something I had never done before, even if it meant me throwing away everything I worked so hard for.

NBA All-Star weekend in Cleveland was approaching. For someone in my role, this was the event of the year to see and be seen. It was the place to be. There was so much I could get done in a few days. I could catch up with my former coworkers from the NBA league office, spend time getting to know Peter away from the office, catch up with peers from teams across the league, and meet with existing and prospective clients. In other words, it was a schmooze fest. All Star 2022 was the first weekend I would attend in my new capacity as executive vice president at the Bucks. It was my coming out party.

All signs pointed to this being another notch in my belt to show that I had "arrived." I was ready to "own" the role I had earned. Attending was not only expected, it was praised.

As I was breaking down to April, I decided I needed to pause and reflect, get back to zero, and refill my cup. So, I focused on a different type of schmooze fest, said no to All-Star weekend, and planned a solo trip to reconnect with the most important person who had been neglected for far too long—me. I agonized over what a decision like this would mean for my career. But, for the first time ever, I valued my mental wellness over my career. I had been on autopilot. I was existing. My compulsion to be the best, the pursuit of perfection, and the surging emotional tax burden had finally broken me.

Instead of going to Cleveland, I booked a four-day solo-trip to a cottage in South Haven, Michigan, a small quaint town on Lake Michigan. It was a three-and-a-half-hour drive from Milwaukee. I was very intentional about the location. It needed to be a place where I could drive to versus flying. On flights, there is Wi-Fi, laptops, and an opening for me to check emails and obsess about what I was missing. Driving, on the other hand, gave me the excuse to sit with my thoughts, listen to music, call people I hadn't talked to in a long time, and so on. In other words, I could do a million things other than work. I purposefully chose a place in the middle of nowhere. It had spotty Wi-Fi, a Wal-Mart Super-center, and few other distractions. It would be the perfect place to reflect, reset, and recharge.

That was the somewhat easy part.

The hard part came when I had to muster up the courage to tell Peter I would not be attending All-Star. It took me days to get the words out. The internal battle was strong.

How would I be perceived?

Would I fail the test of leadership by not pushing through whatever was troubling me?

What would I even say?

Could he possibly understand what I mean when I share the struggles I'm having?

How honest would I want to be?

I came out of that battle realizing that I didn't have to share anything I didn't want to. It wasn't Peter's business to know why I was struggling. I had earned the time off.

After days of procrastination, during a regularly scheduled weekly check in, I just said the words. "Peter, I'm going to skip All-Star weekend and head out on a solo trip to South

Haven, Michigan. I need to take a step back and get some rest before the second half of the season." His response was nothing I had expected. He simply said, okay and asked where South Haven, Michigan was. We moved on to the next topic on our agenda.

Just like that. The battle I had in my head ended up not being a battle at all. Wow.

Thirty-six days after my conversation with April and twenty-four days after Peter's sign off, I packed my bag and headed to Michigan. The drive alone was peaceful, filled with music and tears, and full of gratitude and pain at the same time. This was the first time I'd ever been alone with an intention to focus on my mental wellness.

The cottage was perfect, spotty Wi-Fi as expected. It was February, so Lake Michigan was slightly frozen over, with just enough movement to still produce its ocean-like sounds. After settling in, I bundled up and took a walk outside along the lake's cliffside. My mind quickly went back to the porch swing by the pool with my father-in-law. This was my opportunity to just be. Be present, be still, be grateful, be angry, be sad, be ambitious, and be proud.

That walk set off an amazing weekend. I dug deep and set intentions to change not only my mindset, but my approach.

- Instead of running away from the emotions, I felt them for the first time. I learned how to not only sit in them, but also work through them. Too often, I pushed them down or passed them off as a sign of weakness.

- I changed how I talked to myself when I felt I wasn't performing at my best. One of my favorite Peloton instructors, Robin Arzon, often asks during the challenging parts of rides, "How are you talking to yourself? Talk to yourself like you would a loved one." It was easy for me to change my self-talk when she asked me to, and I wanted to set a personal record on the Peloton. I needed to give the same energy to myself when I was off the bike and in the boardroom. From that moment on, I wrote positive affirmations to myself each morning.

- I redefined what *perfect* was for me. I had been obsessive, ambitious, and competitive. My philosophy was the same as Reese Bobby in *Talladega Nights: The Ballad of Ricky Bobby*, "If you ain't first, you're last" (McKay 2006, 0:04:33). As an athlete, I had also adopted the phrase, "Second place is first loser." I always tried to win, whether it was board games or a game of basketball. I wanted to be perfect. This was clearly not healthy, hence the reason I was sitting in this cottage. I saw success and excellence as the destination and not the journey. I wasn't focused on the small wins along the way. What would happen if I paused and was present long enough to see the bite-size victories that took place every day? I could shift my view of success and enjoy the journey. This was a big one for me. I wasn't fundamentally trying to change who I was; being ambitious and competitive will always be who I am. I just needed to redefine the ambitions and the competition.

- I previously defined self-care as an annual massage received as a birthday or Christmas gift from a loved one. It was their way of gently nudging me to slow down and take care of myself. That clearly wasn't enough. Self-care needed to be an intentional effort. I had to force myself to live in the present with gratitude and appreciation for what I already had, who I was, and why I was beyond blessed to do what I do. It didn't need to be large gestures that took hours of my time. I love a good facial or massage, but sitting for hours doesn't appeal to me. I wrote down a set amount of time that would work for me to dedicate to self-care and all the things that bring me joy, even if I could experience them for a short time. I dedicated thirty minutes two times a week to joy because that was something I could commit to without feeling overwhelmed: reading a book, taking the dogs on a long walk, listening to a podcast, walking to my favorite coffee shop with April, watching a mind-numbing reality show, scrolling the GOAT app to choose my next pair of sneakers. The only rule was no work email or phone calls.

- Rest escaped me. A good night's sleep was something I'd heard about from other people. I was lucky to get four hours of sleep before waking up to stare at the walls until my alarm went off. The herniated discs, endless cups of coffee throughout the day, and multiple glasses of wine before bed weren't helping. Something had to change. When I was at the league office, we wrapped the 2019–20 season still in the Bubble in Orlando. There was endless testing, limited guests accompanying the teams, and no fans. The league's basketball technology and analytics team used the OURA ring, a wellness tool designed to monitor players' temperatures, sleep, and heart rate. The goal was to track these as key indicators of illness if they experienced abnormal swings and fluctuations. I mentioned I'm competitive. I immediately went online to buy an OURA ring. If I was going to get my sleep under control, I needed an accountability partner. What better way to compete than to do so with yourself? It tracked my sleep, readiness, and activity. I watched it like a hawk and followed the guidelines for improving my stats. I started going to bed earlier and limited my wine intake to weekends. The impact was almost immediate.

As I prepared to leave the cottage that Monday morning, I reviewed all my notes. I drew a line in the sand and committed to myself—the person who needed me most. For once, I put myself first and wasn't as concerned about what doing so would mean for my career. This was my first step in prioritizing my mental wellness.

The tears I cried on my way back to Milwaukee were tears of gratitude. I was grateful I had the courage to speak up for myself in one of my most significant moments of vulnerability, grateful I could afford to take this solo trip and do the work to reset, grateful that I allowed myself the grace necessary to fill my cup with sustainable and tangible joy, and grateful that there would be other All-Star weekends.

CHAPTER 10:

RESET AND REINVEST

When I returned from South Haven, I saw the office, my obligations at home, and my approach to work differently. I won't pretend that everything I claimed as "goals" on my sabbatical were enacted immediately. At one point, I felt an overwhelming sense of impending failure because I didn't perform my self-care one particular week. The old Raven would have obsessed about all the moments of missed opportunities, subsequently beating myself up to add another level of unnecessary stress.Butwhen that moment creeped in, I focused on positive self-talk and ways to center the small victories.

Before my breakdown, I was the person who made fun of people and their "positive affirmations." Meditation was for hippies. I never thought I would be the person who looked at herself in the mirror most mornings proclaiming, "I'm a bad ass. I got this!" Or the person who practiced five minutes of mindfulness before I walked into the house after a stressful day at work. I needed to be present for April—separation of church and state.

Each day became easier. I was intentional about building healthier habits brick by brick. When my loved ones told me I worked too much, I was confident that I was making the small strides necessary to improve. I knew they would see the change eventually because the collection of my baby steps would be the solid foundation. Prior to my mini sabbatical, their comments would have caused me to spiral down a rabbit hole, feeling like a failure and not good enough for everyone. Instead, I used my words. I proudly shared how I was attempting to make changes and how they could help. I finally had the tools to feel the feelings and self-correct to hear and acknowledge them. I also remained confident in my ability to stay the course on my path to overall well-being.

I became more focused at work and happier at home. It was amazing what perspective provided. I completed projects faster, communicated to my team more effectively, and separated my work stresses from my home life. I found myself thinking more clearly because I directed my time to the matters directly in front of me. Before, I would think about work at home and home at work. The balance of being present to the matter at hand was challenging. My new tools kept me on track.

These tools were pause, reflect, and reinvest.

During my times of weekly self-care, my mind was less cluttered. On walks with the dogs, I rarely took my cellphone, which left me free to think about things outside of work. I used to check emails or make work calls. On the rare occasions when I did have my phone, I got lost in music or tuned into a podcast that stimulated the parts of my brain that were sometimes neglected. I dreamed more unimaginable dreams.

Sometimes I would question the dream I was living.

Was I limiting myself? Why did I stop dreaming in the first place? Who was I trying to please? What and whose standard was I trying to live up to? I made it clear to anyone who would listen: I wanted to be a team president or CEO and run a sports business at the highest level. That was the destination. I assumed I would do that until I retired, then ride off into the sunset.

Could there be more to the story? Could I achieve more than what I thought was the highest level of my career as I currently knew it? The answer was a resounding yes.

I widened the aperture.

I didn't want to limit myself to being an employee for the next twenty or thirty years. Yes, I still wanted to be a president, but I also wanted more. I believed I could contribute more, but not just for the sake of making money. I wanted to make an impact beyond the bottom line. I had already defied the odds to make it to the senior executive level, generating significant revenue for others. What more did I need to learn and who else did I need to know to do it for myself?

I had to be careful. Previously, when my mind wandered into a "dreamland" like this, I'd obsess about every single step I could take to get to the goal. If I wasn't careful, my type A-plus personality would creep back in and take over, focusing only on big successes versus celebrating small victories.

So I paused to reflect on how I got to this particular moment of wanting more, but also believing that I could achieve more. Then I reinvested in the healthy habits I was learning to build.

As I was adding positive affirmations and self-talk to my vocabulary, I also began to study books about manifestation. In *Manifest Now* by Idil Ahmed, one affirmation resonated with me immediately upon reading it:

"My mind is powerful. I can manifest what I want. I see the vision clearly. It is happening now" (Ahmed 2018, 108).

My vision was shifting.

I was never one to speak negatively out loud. Even as a young kid, my mother taught me about the power of words. Setting and manifesting positive intentions was the next goal to conquer and add to my practice. I had a burning desire to answer all the questions I had about what was next for me, but in a more global sense versus the myopic one on which I had been laser focused. But I quelled the need to answer everything all at once. Instead, I began writing things down and setting intentions. Instead of solely focusing on my professional goals, which were very black and white, I took a step back and turned inward.

How do I want to be remembered at the end of my career?

What more do I need to learn to be a better leader?

What skills am I missing to become a president or CEO?

Whose mistakes can I learn from if I want to be an entrepreneur?

How can I broaden my impact with the platform I've earned?

How can I leave any circle I'm in better than when I found it?

What do I want my legacy to be?

To this point, my goal-setting exercises centered on a tunnel-vision journey to become a team president. I wanted access to the title and the power, yes, but I had fooled myself into thinking the end goal was the actual seat at the table. I didn't stop to think about what I could do with my seat or if I should set up a new table altogether.

I broadened my goals beyond just what I could accomplish besides making other people richer. I was on a quest to become a better human.

As I felt more balance between my work and home life, I added a weekly thirty-minute exercise to write down the biggest ideas to jumpstart the second half of my life.

Team president/CEO

Paid board positions

Author (Hello, check!)

Speaker

Real estate investor/developer

Owner of a nonprofit social impact organization
Owner of a sports team

I was thinking *big*. Most of these ideas crept up at various times throughout my career, but I never had the courage to pursue them. I thought I didn't possess the skills or know the right people to step into these arenas. I thought they would take me off my straight-lined path to my ultimate destination. I was thinking *too small*.

Each week, I wrote tangible steps to get closer to the goal and who I would communicate them to for accountability. Instead of stressing about a timeline and saying, "I want to be an author by the end of the year," I wrote, "Take a writing class to build confidence in my writing ability." Instead of saying, "I want to be a team president by the time I'm forty-five," I wrote, "Identify the gaps and areas of opportunity I need to improve upon to become a better leader."

After I wrote the steps, I vocalized them to people in my support circle. Saying the words out loud made it real and created accountability. I was amazed at what happened when I took myself off autopilot and remembered what it was like to dream with intention.

At one point, my sorority sister, Lauren, and I had coffee to discuss some of the projects she was working on as the CEO of a Milwaukee-based women's professional development organization. One of them was a mentorship program in partnership with Jackie, one of the wives of the Milwaukee Bucks' limited partners and a well-respected philanthropist in the community. Education disparity was a significant barrier for minority and underrepresented children in the city of Milwaukee. My interest was piqued as I understood the role that education played in my journey and the doors it opened for me. So, I asked for an introduction to Jackie.

That connection led to several conversations on how I could become a more influential player in Milwaukee. A nonprofit board role at a local charter school was open, and I pounced. This opportunity would allow me to leverage my platform for the advancement of education in underserved communities. It could also help me add skills to my portfolio on how to serve and add value to a board. It was a win-win. I joined the board, and it became one of the most fulfilling roles I'd ever played.

The flood gates opened quickly, which surprised me. I continued to meet local activists who helped me see the impact I could have if I played a more active role in the Milwaukee community. I went on to join three more boards that connected directly to my passions and helped me develop the leadership skills I was missing.

As a compulsive, now type A minus, control freak, it was helpful to see how my shift in goal setting was paying off. I fed that need to compete with smaller bite-sized wins. I had fewer moments of being overwhelmed. I originally thought I needed to achieve the big wins that garnered the attention of others. I turned my attention toward the efforts that served my purpose.

Before South Haven, I was so wrapped up in what I did for a living and the person who achieved the heights that I set for myself. I struggled to detangle myself and my purpose from the life I had built on the surface. The rediscovery that took place during my solo trip opened the doors to a sense of purpose beyond what I do, allowing me to surrender to and reinvest in a new destination.

A destination that would serve my needs first.

LET'S RUN IT BACK:
PAUSE, REFLECT, AND REINVEST

Mental wellness is overlooked for those in marginalized communities. Being strong is seen as a "badge of honor"—particularly for black women. The mental and emotional toll that climbing the corporate ladder took on me almost broke me. So I took a step back and focused on what I needed to do to "fill my cup." For too long, I had been giving to others without ensuring my mental and emotional well-being was intact. I poured everything I had into my career. I had to collect myself and reinvest in tools to bring me back to center, while focusing on a healthier way to climb to the top of the sports business industry.

The order in which I took the steps was critical. It started with a turn inward. Before I could consider my impact on others, I had to be honest with where I was falling short for myself.

1. Don't wait until your cup is empty. Pause now and think about what you need before it's too late. Find out who you are outside of what you do and pour into yourself as you would others.

2. When I reflected on what I had already accomplished against all the odds, I had already won. Slow down, be present, and celebrate the small wins.

3. As you look to refill your cup on a consistent basis, don't be surprised if your priorities shift. If they do, reinvest and step into it with your eyes and heart wide open. You may find a deeper purpose. Commit to stepping out of the box that you and others may have placed yourself in.

CHEAT CODE 4:
UNDERSTAND THAT POLITICS ISN'T ONLY FOR POLITICIANS

Initially a game I ran away from, I finally came to terms with the need to play politics—my way. I armed myself with the tools necessary to navigate the spaces not built for me, but I did so without losing myself in the process.

In the fourth cheat code, you'll learn how ill-equipped I was entering corporate America. I came in thinking I would be able to "hard work" my way to promotions. When I started in sports, I knew no one in the industry. I didn't know what was right or wrong in terms of playing the game to get ahead, and navigating the political terrain was beyond challenging. I found myself in the arena with people who were born with the tools and resources to play the game. I quickly realized that for me to gain ground and grow in business, I would need to develop those same tools but personalize them to fit me. I needed to find my own rhythm and approach to corporate politics.

The person who says "I'm not political" is in great danger… only the fittest will survive, and the fittest will be the ones who understand their office politics.

—JEAN HOLLANDS

CHAPTER 11:

NAVIGATION
WITH NO GPS

I was grossly underprepared in my first job at the Florida Panthers.

The job was selling tickets. Although it wasn't rocket science, it certainly required a level of commitment to the craft. And I took it seriously. I studied incessantly. Product knowledge was key. Reading the body language of a prospect, adjusting to their various objections, and being quick on your feet were all skills required to successfully close a sale. I practiced my sales pitches over and over. If a prospect told me "no" on the first, second, or third ask, I tried a different technique until I got them to say yes. Or at least, until I felt I gave it my all.

This was another form of competition for me.

Selling tickets in sports was selling pure emotion. No one *needed* season tickets. They needed to feel connected to the traditions of their favorite team, the time spent bonding with family and friends, and the triumph as they controlled nothing but their vocal ability to push their team to a win. My job was to sell that emotion, or paint the picture, so to speak. I enjoyed building relationships with prospective season ticket holders. I listened intently to the joy they experienced when attending Florida Panthers games. As they explained the excitement their children experienced rooting for the home team, I heard nothing by glee in their voices.

The Panthers were a relatively new franchise, having only been in the NHL since 1993. This was 2006. Many of the prospects were snowbirds from the Northeast or Canada who grew up with hockey in their youth. I tapped into their time watching the greats alongside their family and friends; I helped them visualize themselves in what could be their seats ten rows up from the glass or center ice in the upper level. It was their turn to live this experience with their own family and friends game night after game night. I was good at sales, not because I loved selling, but because I loved what I sold—pure emotion.

The work I put into being a good salesperson was all the work I thought I needed to make a name for myself in this industry. Little did I know, another game was being played. Not only was I not playing, I wasn't even in the stadium.

The game of politics was at play.

I grew up in the '80s and '90s. If someone referred to professional women, whether in real life or television, one pictured women in long-sleeved blouses, skirts to her knees, pantyhose, and modest heels. They were "secretaries," not executive assistants, or they were of service to the men in power. They were mostly seen, but not heard. Not much changed with respect to attire in the '90s and into the 2000s, but I did begin to see more women in power. They were lambasted, however, when they were outspoken and ambitious. God forbid, they wore pants with their suits—read: Hilary Clinton. Society taught me that I needed to dress and act a certain way to be taken seriously.

There were unwritten rules.

"Don't show too much skin."

"Don't wear tight clothes."

"Don't drink too much alcohol."

"Be careful outside the office after hours with your coworkers. It doesn't look good if you're the only woman present with a lot of men."

Those last two resonated with me. I fiercely protected my reputation. I rarely hung out with my coworkers outside of work, especially when alcohol was involved. I feared being seen as "unprofessional." Admittedly, I was jealous when I saw others in our company freely being themselves at happy hours, which seemed to happen as often as two to three times a week. During the weekends, they would even socialize at bars to watch road Panthers games, college football on Saturdays, or NFL games on Sundays. There was no way I would be caught out as a black woman gallivanting with all these white males. My battle was already uphill. Why would I want to muddy it with more obstacles to overcome? As one of two women on our entry-level sales team of eleven, I avoided these events like the plague.

My colleagues didn't understand this. I was often called "aloof," "stuck up," and "anti-social." They had no idea that I was just protecting myself and abiding by the patriarchy's unwritten rules.

So, I kept my head down and focused on the work. As a second-generation college graduate, I expected there would be things that I didn't know going into my first job. I just counted on my work ethic to pick up the slack. There would always be people with more marketable and employable degrees from more prestigious schools, or those who knew someone to get the job. But no one was going to outwork me. I came into the office at 5:30 a.m. and left at 6 or 7 p.m. Surely, this counted for something.

Yes, I assumed I was on an equal playing field. We were in a meritocracy. Or so I thought.

As I packed up my things to leave one Thursday evening, I overheard a couple of entry-level sales representatives, Daniel and Asher, talking about their tee time the following morning. The two of them often played golf on the weekends, so I assumed they meant Saturday. The course they were playing on that day was different from the run-of-the-mill public one where they often played. Wherever they were playing this time was thirty minutes away, and it sounded like a magical, unbelievable, and impossible course. They couldn't contain their excitement as they discussed logistics, which included our boss, Jeff.

Daniel recommended a plan to Asher: "Our tee time isn't until 10 a.m. I'll ask Jeff if we can meet for a quick breakfast at 8:30 a.m. From there, we can hop in his suburban and ride to the course."

Asher replied, "That makes sense. After you talk to Jeff, I'll call Phil and tell him the plan. He's easy going and is thrilled that we got him access to the Grande Oaks course."

Phil was a big player in South Florida. He owned and developed several properties in Fort Lauderdale and had just started his own real estate development firm. His business was booming, and he was very well connected throughout the region. Until that point, he had season tickets to every sports team in South Florida—except the Panthers. Asher changed that when he convinced Phil to buy Panthers' tickets for the upcoming season. Bringing him into the fold meant an immediate connection to other successful business owners who had the potential to work with us.

At the end of each day, our boss, Jeff, would come out to get a pulse on how fruitful our sales efforts were that day. He was a great coach in that way. If we had a bad day or didn't sell anything, he didn't embarrass us. Instead, he asked what we learned from the "nos" we received and what we would do differently to turn that no to a yes. If we made a sale, he would celebrate with us but also remind us that tomorrow is a new day with the challenge to replicate today's success. Jeff reinforced that developing our own sales style was crucial to a seller's success. He would always say, "Never try to be anyone else other than yourself. A prospective client will appreciate your authenticity and, likewise, know when you're full of shit."

As Jeff made his way to Asher and Daniel that Thursday, Daniel used the opportunity to talk about their golf outing. My attention went immediately to eavesdropping on their conversation.

Asher said to Jeff, "Phil can't wait to play the course tomorrow. Thank you again for giving all of us this opportunity to play Grande Oaks!"

Jeff replied, "No problem at all. I'm just as excited. This will be a great chance for you and Phil to get to know each other and for us to strengthen our relationship with his real estate development firm. I know he bought tickets for personal use, but I would love to talk to him about how his company could benefit from expanding his portfolio with us."

Daniel jumped in, saying, "I'm so excited. I'm headed to the driving range tonight to get some extra swings in. I don't want to be embarrassed out there. Tomorrow morning, can we treat you to breakfast at 8:30, and then catch a ride with you over to the course?"

Jeff responded, "Of course! I'm looking forward to it. See you in the morning."

They left to hit golf balls and I'm left with, "What the hell just happened?"

On my short drive home, I replayed this entire scenario in my head. What was I missing? While I was studying and preparing to be the best seller, they were starting the weekend early with golf and drinks with the boss and a prized client. While I had my head down, they were practicing at the driving range.

At the time, I didn't know entertaining a client in this manner could be effective. Again, this was my first job in sports. Jeff was an amazing coach and taught me a lot of what I know about being a seller. What he taught me, however, was the hard skills, such as how to get to a decision maker and what to do to overcome certain objections. He taught me those skills during the workday, when I had to share him with ten of my sales teammates. Asher and Daniel, however, were getting something else above and beyond the hard skills. At breakfast, Grande Oaks, and presumably at lunch or drinks following, they were getting the soft skills and on-the-job training that doesn't happen sitting in one's cubicle and certainly wasn't taught in school. They were gaining access.

They were able to take a day off for the sake of building and expanding a business relationship. But it was so much more. The time alone with Jeff at breakfast and on the ride to and from the course would also help them build a more personal relationship. It was invaluable for the two of them to see Jeff interacting with Phil and learning how to approach a sales opportunity in a more genuine and authentic way. Also, because of the coach I knew Jeff to be, he would undoubtedly instruct and train Daniel and Asher on the spot. Their car ride home would be filled with real feedback and lessons learned that could not be duplicated elsewhere.

I was also confused because, on the surface, it appeared to be just a game of golf. Without knowing their intention, I assumed that Daniel and Asher were just young professionals eager to spend time with the boss on a day outside the office. I couldn't even be sure of Jeff's intentions. I was sure, however, that I didn't know how to play golf. If Phil was my client and wanted to go play golf, I would have either had to pretend or Jeff would have to take him out to the course without me. Either way, it would have worked out differently for me because I lacked exposure to the unwritten rules of fitting in to get ahead—to gain access. I had a formal education and multiple degrees to show for it, but I lacked the informal training that gave me entry to the game being played around me.

What was the lesson here? How do I bridge the gap between being seen as someone who gets the job done and the person who needs to connect with the people who would be influential in the growth of my career? I was missing out. I didn't know exactly what to do, but I knew I needed to do something. Being the first one in and the last one out wasn't enough. Being atop the leaderboard and generating sales for the organization wasn't enough. I wanted that face time with Jeff.

In the *Harvard Business Review* article "You Can't Sit Out Office Politics," Niven Postma discussed how people fall into the trap of denying their role in office politics:

"Many of us have a deeply held view that talent and hard work should be all that one needs to succeed. I think what lies at the heart of this belief is that so many of us treat work like school. When we are at school, it is generally a given that if we work hard and master the subject material, we will get good marks and proceed to the next level. In the workplace though, thinking like this is a risk and a mistake because the reality at work is that invisible contributions have no value" (Postma 2021).

She goes on to challenge us to reframe what politics means to us: "Start to be aware of your language and how it is framing your reality, specifically how it frames the way you understand the work environment and how you choose to show up in it. It's almost never about the activity itself, but rather the intention behind the activity and the interpretation and judgment we attach to both" (Postma 2021).

I knew politics were everywhere, but it was such a dirty word in my friend and professional circles. If you played politics, you were considered manipulative, conniving, and untrustworthy. You were someone who only cared about what it took to get to the top. Those who didn't serve a purpose for you getting there, be damned. I didn't want to be a person who others called manipulative or untrustworthy. I didn't want to have to plot or pretend to be something I wasn't to get ahead. I just wanted to do good work. Why should I do more? I was taught that your hard work should speak for itself.

Tuesday of the following week, I signed up for golf lessons.

I couldn't speak to Daniel and Asher's intentions, but I could see a benefit in reframing my view of how I would handle the same situation. If I was going to grow into the leader I knew I could be, politics was a game I had to play.

CHAPTER 12:

PLAYING A GAME OF TAG WITH POLITICS

I was eleven years old when I first realized I was existing in spaces not built for me.

I was geeked about selecting the music for my first ever optional floor routine in gymnastics. As I thumbed through the catalog of cassette tapes, I saw songs like "Wind Beneath My Wings" by Bette Midler, "She Drives Me Crazy" by Fine Young Cannibals, and "Forever Your Girl" by Paula Abdul. Don't get me wrong, I knew Public Enemy and Queen Latifah wouldn't be in the rotation. However, I was hoping there would at least be a song or two available that were more my speed. I knew the songs by Midler and Abdul, but when I wasn't in the gym, hip hop and R&B were more my speed.

If I was going to be at my best, I had to connect with the music. And yes, even at eleven, I wanted to have input and tap into my creative side on my optional routine. The music was a key piece in making the routine amazing. I had to feel it.

Surely, there were other catalogs to peruse.

I walked up to my coach, holding the catalog with disdain, but also hope. I asked, "Janet, are there any other catalogs to review for my floor routine? I don't like what's in this one."

"I'm sorry, that's all we have," Janet replied in dismissal.

Unsatisfied with her answer, I said, "Okay. I'll just bring some music from home."

"No, you can't do that," said Janet.

"Why?" I asked.

Janet couldn't contain her frustration. "Because *this* is the music that we have to choose from."

We went back and forth for some time. I didn't understand. Music wasn't as easily accessible as it is today. Back then, we had to go to stores like Sam Goody's or Turtles to find and buy cassettes or compact discs (CDs). That said, how was music purchased from those places different from the music in this disappointing catalog? Why couldn't I simply bring my music from home? My request was continually denied. I finally relented, but the confusion remained.

And just like that, I began programming my first ever optional routine to "(I've Had) The Time of My Life," by Bill Medley and Jennifer Warnes.

It wasn't until decades later and numerous soul-wrenching therapy sessions that I peeled back the onion on this encounter.

I had been competing as a gymnast with compulsory routines for a few years. Compulsory gymnastics meets were the entry-level competitions to help us build the core competencies in the sport. When I graduated to level six, the first level in which optional routines were allowed, I was coming into my own. The real creativity came at this stage, and my competencies were expanding. For five years, I had been working toward this moment. I watched higher level gymnasts create their routines and witnessed their empowerment and ownership in the way they performed. It was my time.

Or so I thought.

In the end, I had no say. I had to backflip and twirl to Bill and Jennifer because pop music with mostly white artists was the acceptable standard. That standard existed because I was in a world largely managed by and developed for white people. At the time, I was the only black competitive gymnast. I begrudgingly selected a song that was more palatable to the coach choreographing the routine and the audience watching it. And, I had to smile while doing it.

The higher-level gymnasts I watched from afar looked empowered and owned their routines because they identified with the music. From my vantage point, they didn't struggle with the music selection at all as they performed gracefully throughout their program.

This was my first real introduction to the way things worked and how I had to exist in this space to remain visible to those who matter. I had to get comfortable with presenting myself as two different people: one person at the gym flipping to music from *Dirty Dancing* and another person when I was at home listening to Bobby Brown.

It was unsustainable. Subsequently, my love for gymnastics waned, and I quit at fourteen.

But the struggle was just beginning. By the time I got to high school, I was regularly leading two lives—one in school and one at home.

Over time, I became accustomed to living a life as "the one"—one of a few black people in high school advanced placement (AP) classes and then as one of three black pre-optometry students at Auburn University. I'm ashamed to say it now, but I cringed every time my southern accent showed itself during any conversation, even if it was with other southerners. I had conditioned myself to believe the stereotype that the slow drawl of a southern twang meant that I was unintelligent. I was often told that I was articulate, not knowing until later, that "articulate" for a black person was code for "wow, I didn't expect you to speak in coherent and complete sentences."

My existence with family and friends in my "other" life was less taxing. I could be myself—whatever that meant for someone still trying to figure themselves out into early adulthood. My language was relaxed. I could be emotional. I didn't always have to smile to seem "less intimidating" or "less angry." I didn't have to pretend to be interested in what someone was saying when it didn't apply to my experience, or worse, laugh at jokes I didn't think were funny. With people who looked like me, I didn't have to be "on."

Vacillating between the two worlds was exhausting, but it was necessary. As a black teenager in white spaces, code-switching was a way of life. It continued as it became my mechanism of survival as a black woman attempting to climb the proverbial ladder in corporate America. And it was endless.

I checked the mirror three or four times a day to make sure my locs were tidy.

I didn't talk too loud in meetings or fiercely defend a point for fear of being called aggressive.

I constantly reminded myself to smile throughout the day.

I kept myself to a two-drink max rule when I went out with coworkers.

I ignored microaggressions to avoid being known as someone who plays the race card.

I agonized over clothing and if I was professional enough.

I avoided African-American Vernacular English (AAVE).

I did this all to be seen as more palatable and easy to work with. It was exhausting.

Harvard Business Review's article "The Costs of Code-Switching" by Courtney L. McCluney, Kathrina Robotham, Serenity Lee, Richard Smith, and Myles Durkee defines code-switching as adjusting one's style of speech, appearance, behavior, and expression in ways that will optimize the comfort of others in exchange for fair treatment, quality service, and employment opportunities. They identified three key reasons why black employees feel the need to do this in the workplace:

1. For black people and other racial minorities, downplaying membership in a stigmatized racial group helps increase perceptions of professionalism and the likelihood of being hired.

2. Avoiding negative stereotypes associated with black racial identity (e.g., incompetence, laziness) helps black employees be seen as leaders.

3. Expressing shared interests with members of dominant groups promotes similarity with powerful organizational members, which raises the chance of promotions because individuals tend to affiliate with people they perceive as similar.(McCluney et al. 2021)

I had been adjusting my style of speech and behavior since I was eleven years old. The emotional and psychological toll it took on me was damning. I had been playing politics without even knowing it. What was worse was that I was playing the game with people who were born with the tools and resources to master the sport, leaving me to play catch up.

I was reminded of that game as Asher and Daniel prepared for their foursome with Asher's client. Face time with Jeff would be valuable to them in more ways than one. Better sales leads, advocacy for promotions, and invitations to more outings with clients quickly followed. There were meetings after meetings where they caught up on personal matters. Their connection was authentic. They just understood each other. It sucked to be left out and worse, to know that being left out could hinder growth in my career.

I had to get in on the action, but I didn't want to lose myself in the process. Being fake was not an option for me. I had already taken up golf lessons, but that wasn't enough. To play this game at the highest level, I needed to reframe it. At this point, I knew the experiences that shaped the first quarter of my life negatively affected my view of politics. I was not alone, at least according to Niven Postma, leadership, culture, and strategy facilitator for Niven Postma, Inc, and author of *Harvard Business Review*'s article, "You Can't Sit Out Office Politics." In the article, she explains an exercise that takes place in her workshops and addressed the myth of people associating politics with being a bad person. She asked attendees to provide three words associated with office politics. One hundred percent of the time, 99 percent of the words given are negative. "Toxic," "frustrating," "dangerous," "demotivating," "draining," "unfair," "unnecessary," "cliques," and "gossip" almost always rise to the surface (Postma 2021).

If asked, my three words would have been: gross, stupid, and unfair.

But I asked myself, "How can I reframe this to play it with integrity and without selling out?" I also came to terms with what would happen if I didn't. I most certainly wouldn't have reached the executive levels I've reached. I definitely wouldn't have survived in the sports industry. I wanted to be recognized for my competence and hard work, but I also needed to fully understand the political landscape of both my organization and the industry.

I had to play the long game. Although each stop on my journey at different teams was important, I wanted to become proficient in navigating the politics of the industry. The politics of the sports teams were a microcosm of the industry. It was not only who you knew: It was who knew you *and* who was willing to speak up for you to their peers across the industry. To master the short game along the way, I had to provide a reason for people to notice and speak up for me.

I knew "what" to do, but I still struggled with the "how."

Shortly after the situation with Asher and Daniel, I was desperate for information on how to do this respectfully. My mission began. This was 2006, so this mission looked a little different than it would if I had to do it today. I couldn't just google "How to Navigate Corporate Politics for Dummies." So, I had to get in my car and drive to an actual bookstore. I went to Barnes and Noble to get my hands on every "how to" business book I could find.

I wasn't really sure what I was looking for until I ran across a book by Kathleen Kelly Reardon, PhD called *The Secret Handshake: Mastering the Politics of the Business Inner Circle*. Kathleen Reardon was a professor in management at USC's Marshall School of Business and expert of office politics. I opened it to the table of contents, and the first thing I saw was the chapter "Knowing Your Political Style - and When To Change It." While in the store, I read through the first few pages of that chapter. Maybe this book could shed some light on what was happening around me and how I could navigate spaces to get where I want to be while remaining myself?

In *The Secret Handshake*, Reardon described the characteristics of the four respective players: purist, street fighter, team player, and maneuverer.

- Purists believed in a true meritocracy. Their focus was on being rewarded for their hard work, talent, and being great at their job. Actually, they despised the word politics.

- Street fighters "played the part," keeping tabs on whatever "the part" was that they needed to play to advance. They believed in quid pro quo and helped only those who could be of service to them. They did whatever it took to play politics and achieve success.

- Team players put the team first. They focused on success through the lens of team success, not individual success. They leaned on their interpersonal skills to get the job done.

- Maneuverers would sell out their own mothers if it meant achievement for themselves. Words like deception, saboteurs, and destroyers were used to characterize them. (2001, 22–30)

I was a purist and a team player at heart. After all, my mother and father taught me that hard work paid off, and being "excellent" was both the task and the result. Being a former athlete, playing and winning with a team was a mindset I developed early. As I read this, I thought, "Okay. Maybe there will be some tangible things that could help me here." So, I bought the book and headed straight home to read, highlighter in hand.

The Secret Handshake had some good nuggets in it, including mention of how one's political style could be more or less effective depending on the type of politics being played at one's organization.

But overall, something was missing.

The book didn't speak to me as a black woman and the specific politics *I* had to play when I walked into the office. I didn't want to be a sales representative forever. I aspired to lead people, but I also faced obstacles that my white colleagues didn't face, including:

Exhaustion from existing at work to fit the model of success with "executive presence."

Dealing with microaggressions like comments about my dreadlocks or southern accent.

Not knowing the "right things" to give my energy to outside of just doing good work.

I felt like I was almost back to square one. I continued to search for help and guidance, but I was on my own. There was little in the way of resources that spoke directly to the challenges I faced as a minority three times over. I was looking for the blueprint, but it was nowhere to be found.

Becoming politically savvy would have to come through trial and error.

CHAPTER 13:

DOING IT MY WAY

I played basketball in high school. I was a varsity starter as a freshman with a vertical leap of thirty-four inches; thank you, gymnast thighs. Despite being five foot four, I loved tussling in the trenches to grab rebounds, which in turn led to my nickname, "Mighty Mite." My coach, Jim Holland, gave me that name. I'm not sure if he was trying to say Mighty Mouse, but somehow the nickname stuck.

I was a two guard on paper, which meant I was supposed to be a shooter first. I missed the memo. As a freshman, I had other plans that didn't involve shooting. I wanted to get near the rim to steal rebounds. It took a while for Coach to appreciate this about me. When I began playing for him in the ninth grade, he consistently yelled at me to "Stay out of the lane!" "Shoot the ball!" was also repeated quite often. Especially when I would give up a shot after a perfect pass at the three-point line with my defender several steps away.

"Shoooooooot!" he would yell as he saw the hesitation with the defender closing in.

"Raven, why aren't you shooting?" he asked in the next timeout huddle.

"I don't know Coach!" I'd respond, nervously.

"Are you waiting for Christmas? Shoot the dang shot, or you'll be sitting right here on the bench next to me!"

That shook me. I wanted to play all thirty-two minutes of every game. How could I contribute on the bench? Remember, I hated to lose more than I loved to win. Coach Holland knew what would set me straight. I never wanted to sit out of the game. He said the magic words to make me shoot, much to my dismay.

I picked up basketball in eighth grade after I quit gymnastics. It immediately became an obsession. My dad's twin brother, Walter, was a star high school basketball player and the only person I knew with a basketball hoop in his driveway. My cousin, Steven, Walter's son, was my age and hoped to take the baton from his father as the next great basketball player from Tuscaloosa. One day, during a family barbecue at my uncle's house, my cousins—all boys—were playing basketball as they waited for the call to eat. Ever the tomboy, I went over to ask if I could shoot around with them. They laughed of course and said no.

So, I waited.

They wrapped up their silly game and went over to grab their plates. Instead of eating, I picked up the ball and started shooting. I thought, "What's so special about this game?" I say this with as much humility as I can muster: It came much easier than I expected. At first, I shot right under the rim—really close. I wanted to get comfortable with the weight of the ball, mechanics of my form, and angles of the shot release. It was my introduction to the layup. I moved farther and farther back to shoot from the side, then the free throw line. I missed a lot, but I enjoyed the process of correcting myself to make the shots. Always the competitor, I began playing a game with myself: Shoot and make five in a row from this spot. Then this spot. It was addictive.

Time passed and I missed the calls to dinner. Better said, I didn't care about dinner.

I'm not sure how long I was out there, but food was consumed, fellowship commenced, and family members had come and gone. All while I was out in the driveway with this silly ball.

What happened next changed this game to an obsession in an instant.

My uncle and dad came out and started shooting with me. My dad was good. He wasn't blessed with my uncle's height of six foot four, but he could shoot the rock from anywhere. Before I knew it, they were passing me the ball and coaching me on technique, angles, and dribbling.

"Take your left hand and put it here, then your right hand goes here," my dad said as he instructed me on the shoot versus push technique I had been using.

"Yeah. You want to shoot it, not push. When you push, you're not giving the ball a chance to get to the hoop. Shooting allows you to have better control," said my uncle.

"Stand right here and shoot the ball ten times. Tell me how the ball feels leaving your hand after each shot. Was it easy? Did it feel good?" asked my dad.

After the first shot, a miss, I replied with disappointment, "That sucked."

My uncle replied, "Sucking is a result, not a feeling. How did the ball *feel* leaving your hand?"

"I pushed it," I said.

"Good. That's good. No one says I'm going to 'push basketball' when they pick up the ball. They say, I'm going to shoot. Shoot it!" my uncle said.

I shot nine more times and by the seventh time, I had developed a comfortability with the shot mechanics. The joy I felt playing with them and learning from them was immeasurable. This moment with my dad and uncle was priceless.

It not only jump started my love for basketball, but also my work ethic on and off the court.

Within weeks, my mom and dad found someone to pour concrete and erect a hoop in our driveway. After that, I was out there every single day and night shooting until the hoop disappeared in the night sky. When my dad pulled into the carport after a long day at work, I would pass him the ball and he'd put up a few shots with me. With his shirt and tie still on, he coached me along the way. We bonded, and I felt closer to him than I ever had before.

I tried out for the eighthgrade basketball team and made it. My coach, Harold Boddie, made me a shooter right out of the gate, a two guard. I was fine with that because when I wasn't shooting on my driveway hoop, I was watching the Chicago Bulls games on television. Michael Jordan was a two guard. It was 1992. Who wasn't trying to be like Mike? Naturally, this designation as a shooter meant I was destined to be the first female Michael Jordan, right?

At our first practice as a team, however, the plays we ran didn't look anything like what I saw Jordan and the Bulls run. My role as a shooter on this team meant I would mostly be a set-up shooter or come off a screen, catch the ball, and shoot. I wasn't really allowed to dribble or create a shot for myself.

For my entire eighth grade season, I did what I was told and just shot the ball. This was the first time I was part of a true team sport. I loved my teammates. Most importantly, I hated to lose. If I had to "stand and shoot" to get the win for our team, that was all that mattered.

I thought it would be different when I moved to varsity in the ninth grade—new coach, new teammates. Nope, it was more of the same. I wanted to be more involved in the game. I had the frame of a mini body builder and three times more boy cousins than girl cousins. I could take a few bumps and not be phased by a little rough and tumble action. Coach

Holland loved the intangibles, but he especially loved the defense and rebounding. So instead of running out on a fast break after a change in possession as most guards do, I started sneaking in the paint on defense to grab rebounds.

During driveway sessions, my dad taught me how to predict the angle that a ball would come off the rim based on its trajectory. He purposely threw errant shots at the rim for me to rebound. It was about being in the right place at the right time. I had a knack for being in the sweet spot.

I had success rebounding on both the offensive and defensive ends as a five foot four guard. I struggled with just shooting and staying out of the paint. Knowing my strengths, I felt I could contribute more to my team. I wanted to convince Coach Holland that I could add value and differentiate myself from the other guards on the team.

Enter politics and negotiation.

One day after practice, I sat down with our assistant coach, Coach Boddie—yes, my eighth grade coach—and asked him why I couldn't do more on the court.

In the sincerest, most eloquent, and humble way a fourteen-year-old could have a conversation, I asked, "Coach, why is my *only* job to shoot? I know I'm not as good off the dribble as Channing"—our point guard—"or Nikki"—our off-guard—"so I get that you all don't want me dribbling. But I can do so much more than that. I want to do more for the team."

"What do you mean, Raven? We all have a job, and your job is to shoot," he replied.

"But can't I have more than one job?" I asked.

"Well, your other job is to play defense. That will keep you on the court and off the bench. You know Coach Holland loves defense!" he replied, thinking that what he just said was some enlightening moment.

Initially annoyed with the response, I saw an opening and opportunity to connect some dots.

Maybe, just maybe, the door would open for me to be more active on the court if I could show them that I could do the basics well—play defense and shoot.

"Okay, Coach. How many shot attempts do you all want me to have per game?" I asked.

"Well, it's not about the number of attempts, it's the number of good shot attempts," he replied.

Duh. I knew that.

Sarcastically, I asked again. "How many *good* shot attempts do you all want me to have per game?"

"Fifteen to twenty," he replied.

"Great. Thanks Coach. See you tomorrow."

My fourteen-year-old brain began racing toward rationalization. I thought if I did my core jobs well, I could negotiate more time doing the fun stuff like grabbing rebounds.

I ratcheted up my efforts. Every practice after that conversation with Coach Boddie, I focused on my defense, and I shot the ball every time I was open. It was awkward at first because my inclination was to run to the basket for the rebound every time the ball was shot.

My freshman season was all about doing what Coach Holland told me to do. I wanted to show him that I was coachable and a team player above all. Over the summer, I continued to work on my footwork, especially on defense, and began focusing on shooting off the dribble.

And I still practiced rebounding my dad's errant shots.

By the time my sophomore season rolled around, I had established a good amount of equity with the coaching staff. I was prepared to put it all on the line and go to work on "the boards"—a.k.a. rebounding. I was confident in my preparation. My value proposition would prove to be both beneficial to the team and help me to become a more well-rounded player.

Our team executed two drills at every practice—three on two defensive drills, and two on two box out rebounding drills. We never knew when the drills would happen. But I knew whenever they did, I would be ready.

And it happened.

It was the end of practice. With thirty minutes left and everyone exhausted, Coach called for both drills to happen back-to-back. Up first was the two on two box out rebounding drills. This drill was designed to teach "boxing out," a technique where the defensive player places their body between the basket and the offensive player to prevent the offensive player from getting the rebound. The entire team took turns playing the offensive and defensive roles. Two players on defense guard the two on offense. Coach shot the ball, and the battle for the rebound began.

It was my turn. I started on offense.

The shot goes up, and my defender, Nikki, a senior who was three inches taller than me, did her best. I maneuvered to the basket, eyes never losing sight of the trajectory of the ball, grabbed it near the rim, and put it back in the hoop. Score!

"Again!" Coach yelled.

Shot goes up, same result.

"Nikki, how many times are you going to let this mighty mite run over you to get the rebound?" he yelled.

Coach shoots the shot again, and again, and again.

And again, I kept my eyes on the ball and grabbed the rebound. I was in a zone but feeling bad at the same time. I didn't want to make Nikki look bad, but the drill was designed to make us all better. She was one of the upper-classmen who had welcomed me with open arms as a fresh-man on the varsity team. Our teammates respected her. They followed suit when she treated me with respect even though

I was the baby of the group, still learning how to play this beautiful game.

Each time Coach yelled at her, I looked back at her and said I was sorry. I was still one of the youngest players on the team and didn't want to be viewed as the teammate who was only out for herself. So, when the ball went back up again, I didn't go as hard and let the other two fight for the rebound even though I knew I could have gotten it.

Coach saw right through it.

"Raven, you're not doing anyone any favors by pulling back. Don't ever let up!" he yelled before ending the drill, and subsequently practice.

Confused, I thought I had ruined everything. I thought my teammates hated me, and I knew for sure that Coach thought I was slacking.

This was not working out the way I thought it would. My dad picked me up from practice, and I cried all the way home. He tried his best to console me, to no avail. When we got home, I skipped dinner, took a shower, and stayed in my room. I didn't come out until the morning when it was time for school. I didn't want to go. If I did, that meant I had to go to basketball practice and face the consequences for being a selfish teammate. According to the school rules, if I didn't attend classes, I couldn't attend basketball practice. So, I told my mom I was sick.

I sulked and tried to forget the disaster of the previous day.

The following day, I walked into practice hesitant and timid. To my surprise, the first person to greet me was Nikki. She asked if I was feeling better and said she missed me in practice. I was thrilled to hear that at least she wasn't upset about how things went down two days ago. Maybe I was wrong about how everyone felt about me.

We warmed up and practice ensued. I laid it all out on the line as we battled the second string. This was my first scrimmage since making up my mind that I would try my hand at rebounding again. I didn't hesitate despite the scary feelings I had coming to the practice. On one play, I was on defense. The ball was shot, I grabbed the rebound and started a fast break. The other two guards joined me as we faced a sole defensive player. It was three on one. I passed to the guard on the wing, and she passed it down low to the guard below the basket—score.

We ran it back with the same result.

A man of few compliments and even fewer smiles, Coach Holland beamed from ear to ear as he approached Coach Boddie. The two of them whispered to each other. They realized that my rebounding and subsequent speed could start a fast break. It added a new element to our offense. Before that, we were a traditional half-court set up offense that prioritized higher percentage shots near the rim. Our pace was very slow. This new element allowed us to take advantage of the speed we had on our team. We were a well-conditioned team. This also meant we could push the tempo, causing other teams to tire more quickly.

Instinct met preparation. My trade off worked. Coach Boddie was my advocate along the way, keeping me focused on the things that mattered, like shooting and playing defense. Because of his guidance, I built equity with Coach Holland and earned enough performance currency to try new things. I learned from my missteps but continued to believe in the ways I could add value to the team.

How did this very long story about my glory days in high school help me with corporate politics?

I replayed this time in my life after reading Reardon's book. I was searching for answers to how I could play politics my way. My high school basketball experience came up when

I reflected on how I turned challenging situations into winning ones. I was up against a similar situation as I watched Daniel and Asher gain favor and access to opportunities that I wasn't privy to. It wasn't that I was underprepared to play the corporate politics game. It was that I was trying to play it the way they were, which was never going to work if I wanted to remain authentic. I didn't have the same tools they had, so I had to create my own.

My approach to gaining access to advancement opportunities in corporate America had to be like my approach to showcasing the full breadth of talent I had on the basketball court. And this would take more than learning how to play golf and attending happy hours after work.

I broke down the steps of how I was able to convince our coaching staff that I could do more than just shoot.

- **UNDERSTAND THE ORGANIZATION:**

I knew what mattered most to my coach: defense was first, shooting was second. If I did those things, the basics, I could get his attention and earn more playing time because I was adding value on both offense and defense.

- **KNOW MY UNIQUE VALUE PROPOSITION:**

It was clear. I was a shooting guard, so my job was to shoot and do so often. Aside from that, I focused on the intangibles—the things that didn't make the stat sheet at the end of a game but earned respect from my teammates and coaching staff. I showcased the unique value I brought to the team: my hustle, work ethic, going all-out on running drills, and being vocal as a leader even as a freshman.

- **INVEST IN SOCIAL CURRENCY:**

That respect was my social currency. When I thought I embarrassed Nikki, it was my social currency that gave her the confidence that I was always a "team-first" teammate. She was the first one to welcome me back to practice because she knew the value I added and that my intent was always to make the team and my teammates better.

- **BUILD UP MY PERFORMANCE CURRENCY:**
I continued to add to my performance currency, never being satisfied with just playing good defense and shooting. I could have stopped the rebounding drills with my dad, but that would have limited what I could do on the court. Being relentless to perfect my craft and adding dimensions to my game is what eventually helped me gain the trust of my coaches.

- **FIND A MENTOR AND AN ADVOCATE:**
Coach Boddie was my guide the entire way. When I first went to him to complain about not being able to rebound and *only* being allowed to shoot, he basically told me to "shut up, do your job, and shoot." But he also shared that Coach Holland loved defense. Had I not focused on those two things, I would not have continued to start for an eventual state championship team.

I took a step back. These five principles, if applied to my career, could help me make sense of the political game I needed to play as a black woman trying to thrive in corporate America. Through trial and error, my approach was methodical and intentional.

- **UNDERSTAND THE ORGANIZATION:**
In Kathleen Reardon's *Harvard Business Review* article "Office Politics Isn't Something You Can Sit Out," she describes the levels of politics in organizations—minimally, moderately, highly, and pathologically political (2015).

- Minimally—what you see is what you get. The culture is built on transparency and camaraderie. Standards for promotions and expectations for leading and managing are made clear. This is the type of organization that those not interested in politics could thrive in.

- Moderately—politics exist here but go largely under the radar. Conflicts are unusual because there is a team player mentality. This type of organization can be easily navigated if one can participate in pockets of political activity.

- Highly—who you know is more advantageous than what you know. Not understanding or playing politics in this organization can exact a price and one will be left behind. "In groups" and "out groups" exist with those who are "in" having proximity to power and a better chance of knowing what it takes to climb the ladder.

- Pathologically—this organization is built on a toxic and fractional foundation. More time is spent watching one's back than working, and people are distrustful. (Reardon 2015)

The level of politics in the organizations I've worked for has been wide-ranging. Before I could develop a plan for being recognized for my efforts and growing within an organization, I needed to know what level of politics to play. I spent the first three to six months learning, listening, and taking the pulse at every company I've worked for.

Who commanded the room in meetings?

Was there a certain language that resonated within those meetings?

What was the body language of others in the room when certain people spoke? Was it dismissive or attentive?

Who gathered around the "water cooler" and what did they discuss?

Were there meetings after meetings with people staying behind to chat, and who were those people?

Who did the "boss" go to lunch with or hang out with after work?

I tried to pay attention to the unspoken languages that took place in corporate settings. Although uncomfortable, it was necessary. Then I executed.

• **KNOW MY UNIQUE VALUE PROPOSITION:**
My work ethic has never been questioned. I was not going to be outworked. However, that wasn't enough. As I watched Asher and Daniel gain access and exposure outside the office and on the golf course, I needed to tap into what made me stand out as a seller, and eventually as a leader. I refused to take on the "used car salesperson" reputation that saddled some sellers. Instead, my sales approach was listening more than I spoke, painting a picture, and selling emotion. As I mentioned before, no one needed season tickets. So, I leaned into my relationship-building skills to build trust first. That set me apart from the other sellers who promised a certain return on investment or sold features. That skill translated into my leadership. I lead from a position of service and empathy. If I asked my team to do something, I did it alongside them. I was in the trenches with them and treated them as individuals, never painting them all with one broad brush. Because I built relationships with each person, I knew what it took to get the most out of them and tap into what made them unique.

Differentiation was the key. I not only had to understand what made me uniquely qualified to do a job, but also learn how to communicate that value. I went deep to understand what made me uniquely qualified and earn the promotions I received.

- **INVEST IN SOCIAL CURRENCY:**

The respect I garnered from both my clients and colleagues was the foundation for building solid relationships throughout any organization, regardless of the level of politics. I initially avoided personal relationships early in my career, thinking that no one needed to know me outside of what I brought to work. Although I didn't open up to any and every one, I did open up. I was selective but intentional. I joined company softball and kickball teams. I went beyond the obligatory "good morning" and asked about their weekend. I asked about colleagues' kids and took an interest in their hobbies and extracurricular activities. I sought out travel recommendations from those who made the most of their time out of the office.

I was looking for a thread. What could I have in common with a coworker to help build an authentic relationship? Who would be the person who would talk the least about work if we grabbed a drink on occasion? Whose significant other would April enjoy hanging out with the most?

Investment in and with social currency was vital to navigating corporate politics. However, I was adamant that I never wanted to do it for the sake of survival. I'm friends with many of my former coworkers because I was determined to connect with them in an authentic way.

- **BUILD UP MY PERFORMANCE CURRENCY:**

I never stopped perfecting my craft. The craft changed, however, as I traversed the leadership journey. I was no longer just focused on what I brought to the table. My responsibility was now to my team and the person I reported to. I had to make them all look good, while also developing both my soft and hard skills. I read books on leadership for inspiration, with Simon Sinek's *Start with Why: How Great Leaders Inspire Everyone to Take Action* leading the way as a book that transformed how I wanted to be viewed as a leader. This quote jumped off the page:

> *"Great organizations become great because the people inside the organization feel protected. The strong sense of culture creates a sense of belonging and acts like a net. People come to work knowing that their bosses, colleagues and the organization as a whole will look out for them. This results in reciprocal behavior. Individual decisions, efforts and behaviors that support, benefit and protect the long-term interest of the organization as a whole."*
> (Sinek 2009, 105)

Along with Simon's inspiration, I took online courses through Udemy and Coursera to develop skills like project management and strategy building. I raised my hands for the projects that no one wanted to do to capitalize on building skills I didn't possess.

I prepared for the job I wanted as much as I did for the job I had. If I was in a meeting and heard unfamiliar strategies or business language, I'd immediately do research to learn more. Once iPads became a thing, I'd google unknown words in a meeting to at least get a baseline on what was being discussed. It was key for me to take on extra learning opportunities on the weekends and showcase that my skillset was expanding beyond what was on my job description. I didn't need to know everything about everyone's job, but I wanted to be able to speak the same language. This made it a little easier for my advocates to speak to my work when I wasn't in the room. They knew that when they hired or promoted me, I wouldn't simply just do my job. I would always be prepared to do more.

- **FIND MENTORS AND ADVOCATES:**
With both my social currency and performance currency increasing, it was easier to ask for mentors and advocates to support me on my journey. I never wanted to ask for help before I was ready to receive it. In organizations that were highly and pathologically political, both mentors and advocates were a necessity. Mentors helped guide me through potential landmines while giving advice on who and what to know along the way. Advocates spoke up for me and, most importantly, spoke to the value that I could add to the organization. When I felt invisible, they made me feel seen. If someone attached their name to mine, my responsibility was to make them look good and follow through.

Once I established "my way" of playing politics, surviving and thriving in an organization became less daunting. Don't get me wrong, it was absolutely exhausting to have to perform and do all of these gymnastics. But, I no longer looked at this as a game that I was ill-equipped to play. Instead, I looked at it as a necessity—one in which I would play with authenticity.

LET'S RUN IT BACK:
UNDERSTAND THAT POLITICS ISN'T ONLY
FOR POLITICIANS

I worked in spaces specifically designed for those with inside knowledge on how to succeed in them. In those spaces, I found people with multiple Ivy League degrees, well-connected college-educated parents, and tools to navigate corporate America with ease. This was the pool of peers I competed with for jobs. They were born on second or third base. Sometimes, they owned the stadium. I'm a product of a public school education from one of the country's worst states for education. I have two degrees from a state college. My parents didn't finish college, and I had no connections outside of Tuscaloosa. I was born in the dugout. Others who look and love like me may have been born in the locker room. And even more were born outside the stadium. I knew nothing about how to traverse the world I found myself in while also trying to prove that I was more than qualified to be there.

The gamesmanship and politics can be exhausting, but I am determined to hold court in an authentic way with integrity as my backstop.

1. Don't be naive to think that politics doesn't exist in the industry or organization that you're in, want to be in, or will soon be in. The sooner you accept it, the better prepared you'll be to navigate it.

2. I wanted to stay true to myself on the journey to becoming a savvy corporate politician—a journey I'm still on. On several occasions, I had to remind myself that strong integrity and character were the foundations of my values. You will be tested. Once you come to terms with the fact that you have to play the game, remember who you are. Commit to being "you" as you play it. Never let the game play you.

3. Remember the five principles and tailor them to your style:
    a. Understand Your Organization
    b. Know Your Unique Value Proposition
    c. Invest in Social Currency
    d. Build Up Your Performance Currency
    e. Find a Mentor and an Advocate

CHEAT CODE 5:
COLLECT ADVOCATES

Advancement in my career was not based purely on meritocracy. It was not only about who I knew, but also about who knew me. Along the journey, I found advocates who could speak to my unique value and contributions when I wasn't in the room.

In the fifth cheat code, you'll learn about my evolution in asking for and accepting help. It was uncomfortable, but also rewarding. No one at the top made it there alone. I've been fortunate to have amazing advocates who have not only spoken up for me in the room, but also opened doors for me to take my rightful place in the conversation as my own advocate. Without them, a seat at the table would not have been possible.

One hand is never enough to lift a heavy load. A single hand cannot cover the sky.

—AKAN PROVERB

CHAPTER 14:

BUT FIRST, WE ADVOCATE

———

In my first year at the Pittsburgh Pirates, I was asked to manage an eight-figure portfolio and lead a staff of nine senior-level sellers. This was only my second leadership role. It was a stretch—I had never been responsible for a staff this size or a revenue scope this large. Before getting this job, I applied for several others but was rejected for "lack of experience." Leading my new team to success was the goal, but in the back of my mind, I also wanted to prove the hiring managers who rejected me wrong.

I had two goals for year one: (1) meet and exceed the revenue targets set before us, and (2) put processes and strategies in place to make us a more efficient and effective sales team. I coached the team, listened for opportunities to make them better sellers, and delivered on the goals set before us. We had a lot to celebrate.

When it came to my first year-end review, I was pumped to bring that celebratory tone to my boss, Chris. I expected Chris to shower me with glowing words of praise, encouragement, and maybe even a raise. I practically skipped into his office.

"Raven, have a seat," he said calmly. "Congratulations on getting through your first year. Awesome job. You've done everything we've asked of you and more. We're so glad you're on board."

"Thanks Chris. I'm excited about what our team accomplished this season given the odds stacked against us," I replied. We had just completed our eighteenth straight losing season. In fact, during my tenure with the Pirates, we had a losing record three years in a row before breaking an overall twenty-one-year losing streak in 2013. Selling tickets for a team that consistently lost required a certain level of skill, patience, and commitment. Our entire sales team was up for the challenge.

"I agree," Chris replied. "It's not easy day in and day out to come in with the energy that you and our teammates bring every day."

With pride, I beamed. I proceeded to go into detail about the successes of each one of my staff members. "Yes, several people on my team really stepped up to lead the way. Jordan became a de facto leader on the sales floor and kept the team focused and motivated every day. Valerie improved her group sales efforts this year, knowing that was the piece that kept her from hitting her goals last year." On and on, I went.

Chris was voraciously taking notes. He was the kind of leader who wanted to know what everyone brought to the table. He acknowledged and amplified those efforts as he engaged with the sales team. I loved that about him.

He eventually stopped writing and asked "So, how do you feel about your year? What accomplishments are you most proud of, and what do you wish you had done differently?"

I was a little taken aback by the question. Didn't he know what my accomplishments were? Didn't he realize I had personally coached several of my staff to hitting their goals for the first time in their career? Didn't he know I was working with our analytics team to refine our database management processes to improve the sellers' efficiencies? Wasn't he aware of the work we did with the marketing team to build the narrative and value proposition for owning season tickets? We just led our team to one of the best performances in years. My team exceeded their goals. I was their leader. I was happy. Why was he asking me questions when he already knew the answers?

"What do you mean, how do I feel? I feel amazing. We did great this year! I look forward to doing it again next year with an even more lofty goal that I know you're going to throw our way," I replied with a nervous chuckle.

"No, I know you feel amazing. You and your team *did* do great. But I'm asking about what *you* accomplished this year and what areas of *your* leadership do *you* want to improve?" he asked.

My heart began to race, and my brain was scrambled. I had no answers. I hated that feeling of being paralyzed and not knowing how to respond. I looked at Chris's hand—pen ready to take notes, but not moving. We both sat there in what felt like an hour of awkward silence. I had nothing.

Seeing the confused look on my face, Chris broke the silence, first with encouragement, then with a lesson I'll never forget. "It's great that you can speak to every single one of your staff members' accomplishments. That's the sign of a good leader. Advocacy for your team is a big part of your job. So is being able to succinctly, but thoroughly, speak to what you as an individual have accomplished and the value you've added."

"Thank you, Chris. That makes a lot of sense." I got up, not even knowing if we were done with the review, shook his hand, and walked out. I felt embarrassed and ashamed. But only briefly.

His words stuck with me. Never again would I be unprepared to speak to the value I added for an organization, during a performance review or otherwise.

I took my lunch break that day and digested what I had learned.

My boss wasn't a mind reader.

I assumed Chris knew all the strategies and tactics that took place behind the scenes to set our team up for success. I took for granted that he knew the blood, sweat, and tears I put into building collaborative relationships with several internal stakeholders. Some of those encounters were excruciatingly painful. They took a lot of time to nurture, but they ended in a higher level of productivity for the organization. I wasn't one who needed a pat on the back, so I never vocalized what was happening. I took accountability for not communicating or "managing up" so Chris could see these small, but mighty triumphs.

Being vague was worthless.

Adjectives like "great" and "amazing" were fluff for results. Chris was looking for specifics on accomplishments. Why was the team "great"? How did I help Jordan and Val elevate their contributions that season? I needed to speak to how I listened in on Val's calls and immediately followed with coaching and encouragement. I should have shared how I delegated "stretch opportunities" to Jordan as a way to get him exposure to leadership. It was important for me to speak to the details of my efforts in delivering results and not just the resulting actions.

Advocacy for my contributions was equally as important as my teams' efforts.

I appreciated that Chris thought I was a good leader when I advocated for my team. To that point, I wasn't one to "toot my own horn." This was my first lesson in knowing the difference between bragging and having confidence in my abilities.

My efforts were a large part of why my team was successful that season. I needed to own it. I had to speak as loudly for myself as I did for others.

I gave myself some grace. I accepted the lesson Chris taught me that day.

Over the next month, I developed a process to ensure that I would never be caught unprepared again. I created my elevator pitch. It evolved regularly with every new achievement. Additionally, I wanted to develop a process for keeping my résumé up-to-date. I had to speak succinctly, but thoroughly, to that value.

In January and June of every year, I would look back six months, assess my efforts, and break them down into accomplishments, value added to the organization and/or myself, and what I learned or wished I knew. I would then look forward six months and set goals for what I wanted to accomplish and what I needed to learn to improve my chances of advancement, increased responsibilities, and/or salary increases.

I called it *Looking Back to Look Forward*. I needed to be specific in each of the four categories—Accomplishments, Value Adds, What I Wish I Knew, and What I Wanted or Needed to Learn.

Looking Back...

ACCOMPLISHMENTS:

These had to go deeper than results, both when looking back and forward. As a sales leader, it was easy to say my goal was to exceed our annual sales goals. But I wanted to dig deeper. When I looked back on accomplishments, I highlighted specific examples with the characteristics and competencies of my growth in leadership: effective cross-department communication, development of the team I was leading, and creation of strategies that made us a more efficient and effective team.

The key was having clear examples, metrics, and/or data to support these competencies.

When I looked ahead, I established goals that stretched me. For example, selling and leadership came naturally to me. But instead of saying, "Become a better sales leader," I said, "Identify two new sales enablement tools that shorten the sales cycle" or "Implement one new sales best practice that can be implemented in the next fiscal year." The specificity in both scenarios helped me hone in on what was most important because I gave clear metrics and deadlines to hit. It was a game changer for me.

VALUE ADDS:

At first, I confused my accomplishments with the value I brought to the organization. I thought if I hit all my goals and did what was asked of me, I was valuable. When I listed all my accomplishments, however, some things weren't accounted for: my ability to bring varying personalities with even more varying opinions into alignment on one decision, the skill of bringing out the best in my team, the voice I had in the room when pushing for more ethnic and gender diversity on both our leadership and sales teams. These were the skills that didn't make the résumé but were the most important in my becoming a leader—the soft skills.

And here I thought doing my job at a high level as written in the job description equaled my value. I was wrong. The soft skills I brought to the table created culture. They differentiated me from other leaders in the organization and made me uniquely valuable in a way that others weren't. Anyone could lead a sales team to just hit their goals. My value was doing that plus having fun, learning along the way, and tapping into each individual's strengths to pull out the best in them. I wanted to be the leader people wanted to work for.

I wanted to be invaluable.

WHAT I WISH I KNEW:

During my first year at the Pirates, I learned so many lessons—but one in particular stood out. As I was coming up as a seller in the sports industry, it was nearly impossible to get a job in sports if you didn't know anyone. Or at least, know someone who knew someone. It was extremely competitive, which led to a "leadership by fear" philosophy from some leaders. Across the industry, it was understood that if you didn't perform as a seller, a thousand other candidates were waiting to take your seat. It was true. Maybe not a thousand, but there certainly wasn't a shortage of people waiting in the wings for their chance to work in sports.

Unless you asked for help, there was very little hand holding from your boss. The coaching was not personalized, and there was only one way to sell: *be aggressive.* As a young seller, I asked for help a lot and was vocal about not being coached the same way others were. I was fortunate enough to have a boss who was a true coach and pushed me to develop my own style of selling. But that wasn't the case for other sellers I knew in the industry.

For some reason, I forgot about my experience when I became a leader for the first time. I fell into the trap of leading with the same philosophy, through that style of fear. An arrogance about me was unnatural, but I was leading how I saw others lead. Then, when I saw that my team wasn't buying into my leadership, I knew something had to change.

I began spending more time with each of them, getting to know them as individuals. This allowed me to see their weak spots and personalize their coaching. The moment I started treating them as individuals and not painting them with a broad brush, I noticed an immediate change when we gathered as a group in our weekly meetings. They each were more confident, vocal, and engaged.

Had I done this earlier, we may have been able to accomplish more in my first year at the Pirates. However, I needed to learn that lesson to evolve in my leadership.

Looking Forward...

WHAT I WANTED/NEEDED TO LEARN:

I needed to arm myself with both the hard and soft skills to become a better leader. I had to be careful not to push myself to learn too many things or "too big a thing" in one six-month period. For example, I eventually wanted to run the entire sales team, which was Chris's job. But it was unreasonable for me to learn how to manage an entire sales team and the profit and loss budgets related to that team in six months. So, I broke it up into smaller bite-size pieces. I asked Chris if he would allow me to sit in on his meetings with finance as they developed the budget for the following season. This goal was specific, but broad enough to allow me to understand the rationale and process from start to finish.

Because this was my first time doing my "Looking Back to Look Forward" exercise, I agonized over it longer than I should have. I wrote down everything I could think of, but I knew I was missing some of the intangibles. To avoid having to think of everything during one session in January or June, I committed to keeping a running tally during the year. This would make it easier to distill the most important items into my formalized semi-annual list. It helped me establish more confidence as a leader with the intentions to constantly evolve and learn. I really enjoyed the process.

This was vital to helping me advocate for myself. I had real, tangible examples of my performance and intangible skills that weren't quantifiable but deserved to be mentioned. Armed with intentional self-advocacy, I was able to articulate myself more clearly when asking for the resources I needed to do my job at a higher level. My rationale was punchy and succinct because I spent less time talking about the fluff and more time asking for more support to help our business.

I carried the momentum into my review with Chris the following year and nailed it.

Self-advocacy was the first step in understanding how to get the most out of every opportunity I was afforded in this business. If I couldn't speak up for myself or the value I brought to the table, I couldn't expect others to speak up for me when I wasn't in the room. I knew that growing in my career would be more than just who I knew. To truly ascend the ranks, people needed to know my capabilities—particularly when taking on roles I'd never done before.

Advocates were essential.

CHAPTER 15:

MAKING IT WORTH THEIR WHILE

———

My confidence grew leaps and bounds after establishing my self-advocacy process. I was able to speak directly to the contributions I made to the Pirates organization. Before that, I was simply doing the job at a high level and accomplishing goals that others were setting for me and my team. The "Looking Back to Look Forward" exercise opened my eyes to the work I was doing directly tied to my job description. It also helped to identify the value of the work "between the lines"—the portion of the job that was not on paper.

In my second annual performance review with Chris, I was able to clearly articulate that value and what I wanted to learn in the coming months. After that, I noticed his confidence in me grew. To align with my growth opportunities, he and I made a commitment to each other. I would continue to exceed the goals set before me while developing my team. In turn, he offered opportunities to expand my capabilities and learn the pieces of his job that I was missing in my day-to-day. When I asked questions about why we did things or made the decisions we were making, he obliged. He didn't brush me off. Instead, he took the time to engage my intellectual curiosity, knowing that it came from a place of wanting to learn and contribute more to the team.

The invaluable knowledge and skills I added to my résumé paid off sooner than I expected.

During my first two seasons at the Pirates, I was responsible for building the annual season ticket retention campaigns with a success rate of over 90 percent retention rates. This meant that every season, my team was responsible for retaining over 90 percent of our total accounts. In addition to retaining the accounts, we had to also grow the business incrementally 10 percent from this base. For example, if a company had season tickets with us, the objective was to retain them year after year, but also incrementally increase the total value of their account by adding more of our products—additional season tickets, group tickets for a company outing, and so on. In both my first two seasons, my team successfully met and exceeded both of those marks.

After the second season, the head of group sales, Justin, left the organization for an opportunity at the NBA league office. This was a tough loss for me because Justin had become a great friend and confidante. Our offices were next door to each other, so it was commonplace for us to commiserate about our challenges but also celebrate our successes. In fact, our entire sales leadership team was extremely close. The chemistry and culture we built allowed us to reach new heights together.

Chris began the search for Justin's replacement, which turned out to be more challenging than we all originally thought. The sales leadership team took part in prospective candidate interviews. With every interview, the feedback was the same—each of the candidates could lead the group sales team but missed the mark on being a good culture fit. Because we had found a groove within our team, we wanted to ensure the chemistry, collaboration, and culture was not affected. We continued to strike out on candidates. To add to the stress, we were entering a crucial phase of the group sales cycle. We were behind on the planning for the upcoming season. Each day that role sat empty equaled lost revenue.

In an earlier chapter, I shared how Lou and Chris were "my people." They rooted for me. They challenged me. As I recall this particular time, I realize they also advocated for me.

The following Friday, Chris and I had our weekly one-on-one meeting. A typical meeting involved a debrief of the highlights from that week and a preview of the goals for the upcoming week. I treated it as any other touch base with my list of topics to cover. But Chris had something else in mind. After exchanging pleasantries, he dove right in.

"Raven, I've been thinking. As you know, we've had trouble finding a replacement for Justin, and we're losing daylight in our group sales cycle," Chris said.

"Yea, I know. It's been tough. We just haven't found the right fit that can come in, gel with us, and hit the ground running," I replied.

With a level of excitement I hadn't seen before, Chris said, "I'm glad you feel that way. I have an idea. I spoke with Lou"—Chris's boss—"and he signed off on this. We want to offer you the role as director of group sales."

I was stunned.

First, my title at that time was manager. Second, I had no experience leading a group sales team. I was being offered a promotion *and* an entirely new set of responsibilities.

What?

Shock, confusion, and downright fear was written on my face. Chris could see it. He immediately jumped into sales mode as I sat silent across from him for what felt like days.

He went on to explain. "Over the past two years, you've not only done what we have asked of you in your current role, you've taken on additional responsibilities, added tools to your toolbelt, and above all, you've garnered the respect of your peers and your team. When I asked the other sales leaders how they felt about you potentially taking on this role, they didn't even blink. They all said it was a no-brainer."

I sat there, speechless. A range of emotions blanketed me. I couldn't breathe. I was overwhelmed, nervous, excited, and scared.

"Thank you for thinking I could do this job. But I'm not interested," I replied.

Looking back, I can't believe how easy "no" came out of my mouth. But the truth was, I had found safety in my role. I'd gotten into a groove with my team, and I didn't want to fail. If I took on this new role, I could be setting myself, my new team, my boss, and everyone else up for disappointment. Why would I want to take this chance as a young leader still trying to prove myself?

Chris didn't even bat an eye. As a seller himself, he knew not to take the first "no" as the final answer. He said, "Take the weekend and think about it."

I don't even remember leaving his office or really what happened the rest of that day. However, I do remember that Saturday morning talking to Justin, the former head of group sales. I could count on his direct and honest feedback, which oftentimes wasn't what I wanted to hear. That said, he was also one of my biggest champions. He couldn't understand why I would say no to both a promotion and a new opportunity. The only response I could give him was that I wasn't sure why I was being considered, which wasn't a real answer. I was still in shock, but most of it had turned to denial.

I wasn't ready. The excuses came like a flood:

My team would be upset if I left them, which was almost entirely irrational given that "leaving them" meant I would be in an office next door, but I would still see them every day.

I didn't want to go through all the hard work of getting another team to buy into my style of leadership and methods of reaching success.

The group sales team would see through my inexperience as a group sales leader.

As I went on and on about what I wasn't and what I didn't have, Justin asked me a series of questions that turned my gears in a totally different direction.

"Raven, instead of me asking why you're saying no, let me ask you this. After all the prospective candidates you met and interviews you sat through, why do you think Chris offered *you*, Raven, this job and opportunity? Why did Lou sign off on it? Why did I tell Chris that you would be a great new voice and leader for the group sales staff? Why did all your peers agree that you're the person that they want to help support in this new role?" Justin asked.

I didn't answer right away. But I did switch my line of thinking to *how* I could do the job and *why* I was ready to take this step. I began to search for what others saw in me. At the core, advocating for myself and showing up for my teammates and staff had paid off. What was the purpose of doing the "Looking Back to Look Forward" exercise if I was going to shrink under pressure and not take on the challenges I was preparing for?

I simply replied, "You're right. I've been working toward an opportunity like this since I got here. If I'm going to grow my career anywhere, I will have to take chances and bet on myself."

The self-talk that took place during that weekend went up, down, and all around. The people I had surrounded myself with to that point as advisors and friends were with me on the entire ride. This was the first moment in my career when I realized the value of "finding my people." The people who rooted for me and told me the truth, even when I didn't want to hear it. The people who ultimately reminded me of what I worked so hard for and what I was capable of.

I made several calls that weekend. I made one call to a former teammate, Nicole, at the Florida Panthers who was also growing in her career. She was my sanity check. How do I do this with the same level of intensity as my previous role and not lose myself? She reminded me of all the work we both did to get to this level, having never lost ourselves.

Another call was to my mom. Every decision I've made professionally and personally came with the help of her guidance, even if I didn't always take her advice. She was the ultimate cheerleader and always advised me to follow my gut. "What does your 'peace gauge' say?" she would always ask. The "peace gauge" was my intuition. It was a feeling in my soul directing me to a decision that I would ultimately be at peace with. That Saturday, I tuned in to see where the gauge would guide me.

By Sunday morning, I was ready to tackle the "how." If I took this job, *how* would I do it? I made a pot of coffee, opened a notebook, and wrote a ninety-day plan.

The first week, I would reintroduce myself to the staff and set individual off-site meetings with each team member. I intentionally refrained from asking Justin to give me insights on the staff because I wanted to spend the first thirty days getting to know each of them in my own way with no preconceived notions, just a fresh start for all of us.

The first thirty days, I would pour myself into the group sales budgets and sales pipelines. What was working, what wasn't? Who were the star sellers? Who were the teammates who needed more hands-on coaching?

I kept writing and writing. What started as a ninety-day plan, ended as a six-month, twelve-page strategic plan. Along with that plan came a level of confidence that only preparation could manifest.

I was ready.

Throughout that weekend, I had a community of people who took me from a "hell no, I'm not taking this job" to "I got this" in a matter of a few days.

It all started with direct advocacy and being ready to step up to the plate—no pun intended—when they called my name. Chris put his name on the line alongside mine when he went to Lou. He spoke to my capabilities when I wasn't in the room. Justin knew me like few others and leveraged what he knew about my leadership and the work I put in when no one else was watching.

That Sunday, I made a promise to myself. If someone put their reputation on the line to say I belonged at the proverbial table, I was going to make it worth their while. I would no longer just take a new opportunity and "do well." I would make my advocate proud and steadfast in their decision to mention my name.

I walked into Chris's office that Monday morning, strategic plan in hand, and accepted the role of director, group sales—but that was just the beginning.

We got to work as a team, as I began the work of making my advocates proud.

This experience with the Pirates shaped how I approach every single role after that. I established good habits and kept my focus on what worked for both me and my advocates: (Over)Preparation, Results-Oriented, and Self-Advocacy.

(OVER)PREPARATION:

My approach to preparation was always to over prepare, especially when someone recommended me for a new role. I did homework on the job, researched best practices and trends, and always came to the table or conversation with questions that indicated my level of preparation. Once I got a role, it didn't stop. Intellectual curiosity was my best friend.

I've been told I have an "interviewer" communication style, which basically means I ask a lot of questions and rarely give someone the time to ask me any questions. I probed, not just for information, but for an edge. What would make my new boss tick? What was missing from the last person who had this role?

RESULTS-ORIENTED:
Because all my roles were primarily sales-based, it was easier to attribute success to the revenue performance of my sales teams. But that wasn't enough. With career growth as the objective, I also had to understand what success in the role looked like "between the lines." Meaning, what were the pieces of the role that weren't listed on the job description, but could add tremendous value to the bottom line or the organizational culture? Things like hiring diverse talent to bring unique perspectives and approaches to the team, or identifying efficient but effective ways to do business that led to a more productive sales organization. I added items like this to my core competencies, but also had the philosophy that it didn't matter if it couldn't be measured. This was crucial in keeping me focused on the right things and efficient as a leader.

SELF-ADVOCACY:
The "Looking Back to Look Forward" exercise continued and became easier. As my roles increased in responsibilities, it became even more important to speak directly to the contributions I made on the larger organizational scale. I was no longer listing tactics as I didn't want to just be perceived as a "doer." I included strategies that propelled the business forward or changed the way we did business. I wanted to be perceived as a builder and a strategist; one who could lead

the day-to-day, but also take on work that benefited more than just my team.

These tenets served me well when "making it worth my advocate's time" to say my name in the rooms where I wasn't present. I've been fortunate enough to have several direct advocates who took it upon themselves to refer me for promotions and stretch opportunities.

But having direct advocates is just one form of advocacy. The other form is indirect and is of equal importance. These advocates are the people who made me feel seen and were often on the same level as me.

CHAPTER 16:

I ALWAYS FEEL LIKE SOMEBODY'S WATCHING ME

—

Sports is a competitive industry. It's not only difficult to get that first job, it's also hard to stay in it. To grow, learn, and consistently have opportunities that challenged me, I knew I would sacrifice time with family, my social life would suffer, and I would have to move a lot. The moment I made the decision to make sports my career, I was all in, even if that meant making personal sacrifices.

What I didn't know at first was how small the industry was. When I was at the Florida Panthers, my boss knew my new boss at the Pittsburgh Pirates. As I grew in leadership, several of my former coworkers went to other teams throughout the industry. It was imperative not to burn bridges along the way if I wanted to continue to grow and develop in my career.

When I started in the industry seventeen years ago, a good reputation meant maintaining a strong work ethic, being a good teammate, and delivering results. Now, it's called "cultivating or building your brand." I hate that phrase, by the way.

A person as a brand reduces all that they are to a value that can be commodified. Nonetheless, I knew the focus on "my brand" had to be sharp. I needed help traversing the sports business terrain to grow to the level of leadership I knew I was destined for. I needed someone directly speaking up for me in rooms where I wasn't present. But I also needed allies, or indirect advocates, to buoy and amplify my competencies.

This was no more apparent than how I got the job at the National Basketball Association's (NBA's) League Office in 2015.

Once I learned what the NBA's Team Marketing & Business Operations (TMBO) team did, I knew I had to get there. At the Pittsburgh Pirates, my boss's boss, Lou DePaoli, introduced me to this group. Prior to his time at the Pirates, he was one of the first employees in the newly created TMBO department. One evening, we were sitting in his office during one of our eighty-one home games, and I saw a picture of him and David Stern, then-commissioner of the NBA.

"Wow, you know David Stern?" I asked both amazed and confused. As an avid sports fan, in particular a huge NBA fan, I knew David Stern as the person who helped transform the league into a global brand. He was also the person I remembered being pictured with some of the greats—Michael Jordan, Kobe Bryant—as he presented MVP and Championship trophies.

"Yes. I used to work with him. At the league, he created this group to consult with teams and identify areas to improve their business operations," he replied.

"Really? That sounds interesting. What does consulting with NBA teams look like?" I asked.

"The department is called TMBO, short for Team Marketing and Business Operations. We did 'deep-dives' into the practices of each NBA team across all facets of business operations—marketing, ticketing, sponsorship, etcetera.

Once we understood their baselines, we would identify areas to provide best practices and create next practices to help improve their business performance. For example, if one team was a top team in ticket sales performance, we would share their approach and techniques with other teams that needed help in ticket sales. Stern's philosophy was that we could be competitors on the court, but we needed to be collaborative off the court. Having all franchises performing well on the business front would increase the value of the league as a whole," he explained.

"So, teams just gave you access to their 'books' and let you tell them how to run their business?" I replied, confused.

Why would a team let someone from the league come in and tell them what they're doing wrong? It seemed a little Big Brother-ish to me. I understood the reasons to be collaborative and not have "weak links," so to speak. But it felt like it would be an indictment on the team's leadership if someone came in to tell them how to run their business.

"No. When this group was first created, we were not welcomed by every team. They thought the same thing you did— why are these people telling me what to do? Our approach was methodical. Build the relationship first. There was a lot of travel involved because we wanted face-to-face interactions. We needed to see each teams' operations up close. A team visit sometimes just consisted of taking their executive teams out to dinner to get to know them. We wanted to know what was going well as much as we wanted to know what wasn't. Building a repository of best practices to share with other teams was as important. Once we established relationships, it became easier because they trusted us," he explained.

I was beyond intrigued. I hung onto every word. Everything he described was what I enjoyed about sales. Build the relationship, identify the need, and deliver a product that satisfies that need. My interpretation was that TMBO served as the "recommendation sales" arm for the league, but it also provided exposure to all of business operations. Until that point in my career, I was only exposed to ticket sales. But I wanted to know more about the other areas of the business— mainly marketing and sponsorship. If I learned anything to that point, it was to "follow the money"—stay close to the revenue-generating areas of the business.

I began to connect the dots. This path was not only lucrative, it would also lead me to a leadership role.

Lou eventually left TMBO to lead the revenue efforts for the NBA's Atlanta Hawks and now-defunct NHL's Atlanta Thrashers. From there, he became the chief revenue officer for the Pittsburgh Pirates. His experience consulting with NBA teams on their business operations gave him a leg up when moving to the next phase of his career. He was viewed as qualified to lead those respective efforts at the team level.

Having made that connection, I asked him to confirm what I already knew: "Do you think working at TMBO prepared you to do this job?"

Unequivocally, emphatically, and without hesitation, he replied, "Yes!"

I thanked him for the conversation and insight. This conversation changed the trajectory of my career. Before it, I would have been content to have Chris's job, which was vice president of ticket sales, but not anymore. I had my sights set higher: C-level or bust, by way of TMBO.

I developed tunnel vision. I've always been a curious person, but after that conversation, my curiosity was heightened. I knew I needed to continue to excel at my current role. But I also had to parallel a path gaining access to people who could help open the door to TMBO.

This conversation with Lou took place a year before my office neighbor and friend at the Pirates, Justin, left to take a job at the NBA league office on TMBO's ticket sales team.

By this time, the department had grown beyond what it was when Lou was there. It was now a team of forty people with expertise across all the areas of business operations. Having team experience was seen as a plus. Expansion of the department coupled with my experience working for two sports teams meant that gaining entry could be a little easier.

Justin was one of my closest confidantes. He knew my goal was to eventually land in TMBO. Having him "on the inside" was invaluable. He not only introduced me to several people within the department, but also provided me with insights on the gaps I was missing in my capabilities. And he advocated for me to take his position upon his departure from the Pirates.

One of those gaps Justin identified was my lack of connections in the industry. So, when I took the job as director, group sales—Justin's former role—I set out to make as many connections as possible. It was natural for me to start with leaders who worked in the areas of ticket sales that I worked in—season ticket retention and group sales. I wanted to be intentional, but also "giving" during my outreach; I didn't just want to get to know people. I researched the teams they worked for, inquired about some of their practices, and came to the table with practices that were working for us at the Pirates. I never wanted anyone to feel as if I was a "taker" in our conversations. Over that six-month period, I built real relationships with people all over the sports industry, not just baseball. To this day, I'm still very close with many of them.

Shortly after the conclusion of my fourth season with the Pirates, an opportunity came across my desk that I couldn't ignore. The San Francisco 49ers were leaving their iconic Candlestick Park to open a new stadium in Santa Clara. In sports, being a part of a storied franchise and opening a new stadium is an opportunity that no one should pass up. I had an opportunity to create their new season ticket and premium membership program from scratch as they entered this new era. Every fiber in me was pulled toward California, and I left the Pirates to embark on this new chapter.

I was 100 percent focused on knocking this opportunity out of the park. I got to build a team from the ground up. There were many late nights, tears, stresses, and successes, but I continued to keep my eyes focused on TMBO and the tools I needed to add to my toolbelt.

Then one day it happened.

Shortly after we opened Levi's Stadium in Santa Clara in September of 2014, a role in TMBO's retention team opened. I immediately applied. Within a few weeks, I was at the NBA's office in New York City interviewing with the hiring manager. I was geeked. I felt like the interview went well. Actually, I thought I crushed it. I got on the plane feeling confident—maybe too confident.

I heard nothing—crickets.

I called Justin. He said everything he heard was positive. So, I waited, and I waited.

Finally, I got a call from a 201 area code. On the other end was the hiring manager telling me I didn't get the job, but I should stay in touch—ugh.

Deflated didn't begin to describe how I felt in that moment. Discouraged is a better word. I felt as if I did and said everything right. I sat in my pity for about a week or so and got back to work.

It just wasn't my time.

The 2014 49ers season ended and preparations were underway for the following season. I renewed my apartment lease, and threw myself into work.

In early February of 2015, I received a call from Chris, my old boss at the Pirates. By this point, he'd moved on to take a larger role at the New York Mets alongside Lou who was now their number two executive. Working in New York at some point was on my bucket list. The NBA office was there as well, so I took this as a sign that I was getting closer to at least one of my goals. Chris and I spoke about an opportunity that entailed oversight of the entire ticket sales team, which he knew was also a goal of mine. I was pumped! It was a growth opportunity in one of my favorite cities, and I would get to work with two of my favorite leaders. I had no doubt that I would receive the support I needed to be successful. The stars were aligning.

A week after my first conversation with Chris, I received a call out of nowhere from Senior Vice President Brendan Donohue of TMBO. It took me by surprise. I stalked the NBA's website for openings every week and hadn't seen one in TMBO. One of their WNBA account managers was leaving, and he wanted me to come to New York to interview for the vacancy. I was in absolute shock. I always assumed I would come into an entry-level role if I got a job there. This account manager role could lead to *the job* I had my eyes set on from the beginning: the NBA account manager role that Lou started in a decade before.

Here I was sitting with the potential of two very different opportunities from the perspective of both salary and trajectory.

I jumped in with both feet to assess which opportunity would be best for me. People, resources, learning opportunities, personal and professional network expansion—these were all factors I considered as I looked at both short-term and long-term possibilities.

Things moved fast. A few days after my call with Brendan, I was in the office meeting with my potential teammates; some of whom I'd already met in my previous interview for the job I didn't get. Again, I thought the interview went well. This time, however, I didn't get too far ahead of myself. I was even-tempered as I left New York to head back to San Francisco. I also continued my conversations with Chris.

Two weeks passed with continued conversations with the Mets.

One Saturday morning, my phone rang. It was Chris with an official job offer. Everything lined up perfectly. I was excited but wanted to take a minute to really think it through. If I took this now, I'd be telling TMBO that the time is not right. I couldn't imagine saying yes to a job, not giving it my all, and leaving before I accomplished what I set out to do. So, I asked Chris for a couple of days. He knew that TMBO was in the background, but being the seller he was, he made the offer enticing enough that it would be hard to say no to him. As a friend, however, he granted me the time I requested.

Later that day, my phone rang, and it was Brendan.

My heart began to race and I thought, "Wow, timing couldn't be better to tell me that I didn't get the job."

I picked up, we shared a few pleasantries, and he extended a job offer. I was stunned. I don't even remember what he said beyond, "We want you to come join us in TMBO." This was really all I'd wanted to hear for six years after learning what this could mean for my future in sports. I cobbled enough words together to ask for the official written offer and a couple of days to think about it.

I hung up the phone and an overwhelming sense of anxiety came over me. As a type A overthinker, my analysis of the two opportunities went into hyper-overdrive.

Which role am I better suited for now?

Which will stretch me beyond my level of comfort?

If I take the Mets job, will I ever get another chance to work in TMBO?

If I take the TMBO job, will Chris and Lou be upset?

It was a stressful weekend as I laid out all my options and spoke to my closest advisors.

All signs pointed to taking the TMBO role. It was less money and a lot of travel, which would mean time away from my soon-to-be-fiancée. But the tentacles of opportunities that could spawn from this role were almost endless.

That Monday, I accepted the offer from TMBO. A month later, I was the newest WNBA account manager on the roster.

When I finally arrived in the office, I still had burning questions of how I got there. Why was I the one they called before they even officially posted the opening? Fortunately for me, I got the answers almost immediately. Several things had happened behind the scenes, and they started the moment I applied for the first job I didn't get, thanks to those advocating for me indirectly:

- **LOU:**

Once he educated me on TMBO, I set that as a destination on my journey. When I left the Pirates, I stayed in touch with him and provided updates on what I was doing at the 49ers. When he left the Pirates to go to the Mets, I continued to periodically reach out to check in on how things were going with him. I built an authentic relationship with him. I later learned that Brendan reached out to him when I interviewed for the role at TMBO. Remember when I said sports was a small niche business? Brendan previously worked directly for Lou in a previous role. The stamp of approval that Lou gave me was a crucial piece in the puzzle.

- **JUSTIN:**

I've shared before that Justin was one of my biggest cheerleaders. He's reminiscent of the '90s rap artists' "hype men" on the stage, but also a "truthteller" who would call me on my BS. He also advocated for me with both Chris at the Pirates and the Mets, as well as with Brendan at the NBA. I learned that he spoke not only to my ability to do the respective jobs, but the value I could add to the culture. Often, indirect advocates are the hype men for the things that aren't listed in the job description. That's what Justin was for me in this instance.

- **NICOLE AND LILIAHN:**
They were the hiring managers for the role I didn't get when I first interviewed in TMBO. They were on my second interview itinerary for the WNBA account manager role. I was nervous and excited to meet with them. I knew for sure I would "wow" them and make it impossible for them to say no this time. My first week at the NBA, they both told me why I didn't get the first role: I was overqualified. They both gave me a ringing endorsement for the account manager job and admitted this was a better fit for me.

- **CHRIS:**
He was disappointed that I didn't take the job at the Mets. However, he knew my aspirations were to work for the NBA. After I declined the Mets and told him I was taking the offer from the NBA, he immediately called Brendan—his former boss at the New Orleans Hornets—to endorse me for the job. He's been supportive of me every step I've taken in my career since.

I learned three valuable lessons that I've taken on every part of my journey:
- You never know who is watching.
- Don't take for granted the fact that someone is rooting for you behind the scenes.
- Never burn your bridges.

I may have eventually made it to TMBO at some point in my career. However, I can point to the pieces of my journey and the people on that journey who led me there in 2015. I've been blessed to have my reputation lead the way, with others either directly or indirectly advocating for me at every stop.

LET'S RUN IT BACK:
COLLECT ADVOCATES

It wasn't always easy to ask for help or to know who to ask for that help. Once I determined that I couldn't do it alone, I embraced the process. After I became comfortable advocating for myself, I built strong relationships that led to securing my strongest advocates. They played a significant part in the development of my career. They amplified my work, my value, and my contribution to the organization's success. They helped manifest confidence in my abilities and educated me on how to tell my story. Without them, there is no way I'd be sitting where I am now.

1. You are the CEO of your career. No one should care more about it than you do.

   a. Don't take for granted that your boss or your peers know everything you do to excel at your job.
   b. Develop a process for tracking your accomplishments and "value adds," and look ahead to identify areas of opportunity to stretch yourself beyond your job description.
   c. Then, advocate for a promotion, more money, and/ or added responsibilities with clear examples of why you're ready. Evidence-based accomplishments are necessary.

2. If your advocate recommends you for a promotion or stretch opportunity, remember that your work doesn't end there. You must make it worth their while to continue to advocate for you. At the next level:

   a. Continue to prepare and overprepare as if you're just starting out with something to prove.
   b. Remain results-oriented and identify what success looks like with clear examples of how you're going to accomplish those results. Being vague is worthless.
   c. Continue to advocate for yourself with a clear narrative of the value you add.

3. Advocacy comes in many forms. Build solid, authentic, reciprocal relationships throughout your career. People are watching and willing to speak up for you when the time arises. Be ready.

LEVEL UP:
MAKE THE MOST OF YOUR TURN

I wasn't selfish when I got my seat at the table. My goal was and continues to be to leverage my platform and power to make room for others, to call attention to the invisible, and to speak loud enough for the voiceless.

In order to level up, challenge your self to think about the role you can play in someone else's career. What good is making it to the table if you're only making room for yourself?

Being a leader is about thinking of all the others that you can help bring along. Excellence is broader than just you as an individual, but how you bring your true self and really advance others.

—ROBIN WASHINGTON

CHAPTER 17:

THE BEST PART

———

I discovered the cheat codes.

Now what?

The best thing about being in a position of power and influence is leveraging that position to help others. When I started my career, I knew absolutely no one in the industry. And when I did meet people in power, they didn't look like me. I had no idea how to ask for help. As I detailed in this book, I found a way to build a network of supporters, advocates, and challengers to ride with me on my journey—but it wasn't easy.

I wanted to be the person who others learned from, commiserated with, and celebrated with as they began navigating their own journey to their seat at the table. My goal was to speak to and amplify the work of those who are often invisible as they blend into the noise made by those who speak the loudest. The problem was that I learned all of this later in my career. I failed to realize how I could have been helpful earlier.

As the internet made our world smaller and tools like LinkedIn made executives more accessible, I originally hid from the limelight under the guise of being a "private person." For so long, I didn't want to be seen. I just wanted to work, receive the appropriate acknowledgment for my work, and enjoy the fruits of my labor.

It wasn't until recently that I realized I was doing myself, and others, a disservice by staying below the radar. It was one thing to visibly "represent" for the marginalized communities I'm proud to be a part of. It's another thing to mentor others who look or love like you, while personally sharing your experiences and providing a safe space for them to discuss their challenges.

Before my tenure at the NBA league office, mentoring was not a priority. Sure, I connected with a few people who reached out on LinkedIn to "pick my brain" on how to get into the sports business. But I'm ashamed to say I never thought of myself as someone who had much to offer in the way of mentorship. Any conversation with an "up-and-comer" or "wannabe" sports executive was surface-level at best.

That was until about seven years ago.

One of my coworkers from a previous team reached out to me to discuss a situation she was facing at work. It had been a while since we spoke, but she was always positive, a great teammate, and someone I enjoyed working alongside. When she and I finally connected, she bared her soul and we spoke as if no time had passed. She said several words during the conversation that resonated with me.

Those words were: trust, grateful, advice, and mentor.

She and I talked for about an hour. I think I got more out of the call than she did. I felt useful. Every day, I poured myself into my job to achieve excellence. After all, that was the standard. However, after this one call with her, I felt I had a purpose. My life's experience became a tool to shepherd someone else along their journey. I felt real joy because we worked through her challenge together. I helped foster a resolution that she could live with.

My purpose was service.

I realized in that moment that my offering to the world was through my service to others. Mentorship and pouring into others brought me joy. Before that realization, when people asked me what I wanted my next step to be, I was clear in that I wanted the next logical title from where I was sitting. If I was a director, I wanted to be a senior director, then a vice president, and so on. I was thinking linearly and only about what I thought my purpose was. I worked so much that I hadn't stopped to think about the people who would be coming up behind me and experiencing the same challenges.

What good is learning all the lessons we learn along the way if we only keep them to ourselves? If I didn't want to be the "only one"—the only black person, the only queer person, the only woman—I had to leverage my influence to affect change. I had power in my experience. If I could prepare one person to navigate their journey better because of what I learned, then I've served my purpose.

I also had to relinquish the "private person" I had become. Not only did I not want to tout my accomplishments, but I also didn't want people to know more than what they needed to know about me. Keep my private life private. When at work, bring only my professional side to all conversations. I told myself this was only way to be if I was to be taken seriously as an executive. I was an enigma, but not in the cool Beyonce way.

Once I became comfortable with who I was and my unique value proposition, I noticed early career professionals gravitated to me. I recall what it was like when I was starting in the business, and I had no examples to see as possibility. Once I had that conversation with my former teammate, I knew it was my responsibility to not only serve as possibility, but as someone who could provide access to the information I didn't have coming up.

My challenge to anyone reading this book is to be more than a representative of what is possible. It's not enough to just see you "in the seat." From someone else's perspective, they want to know how you got there and what they'll need to do the same.

• DEDICATE TIME TO MENTORING:

Set aside time each month to work with a mentee. Don't wait as long as I did. You don't need an executive title to mentor. Someone else can learn from your experience no matter how little you may have.

• BE HONEST:

It doesn't serve anyone to just share your surface-level experience. Be specific about what you went through and how you got to where you are. You'll find that opening up and being vulnerable resonates and builds a connection beyond the surface.

• REMEMBER WHAT IT WAS LIKE WHEN YOU WERE IN THEIR SHOES:

You will not be able to mentor every single person who wants your time. However, if someone mustered up the courage to come up to you in person and ask for your time, give them the courtesy of acknowledging how hard it may have been for them to do. If it works out for you to connect with them after that encounter, great, but at the very least—be kind.

• SERVE AS AN ADVOCATE:

Take the time to acknowledge the good work of others. You didn't get to where you are without someone taking a chance on you. I know I didn't. When the opportunity presents itself, speak up for those who deserve a seat at the table.

Be the change you want to see and take the time to pour into others. There's room for all of us.

ACKNOWLEDGMENTS

—

Wow! I'm still in awe because I actually wrote a book. I'm even more in awe of the support I've had on this journey to make it happen.

First, I have to thank my mom, Dephrosia, and my dad, William. I won the parent lottery. The person I am today is only possible because of your guidance, your love, and your endless support. Thank you for making me, well, me. Dad, I wish you were here to see all of this, but I can hear you now telling everyone in heaven "That's Little Will right there." I love you both.

Second, I want to shout out my pal, my ace, my baby sister, AJay. My world was made better the day you were born. I was only five, but I knew I had an immediate best friend for eternity. Thank you for being my biggest cheerleader along the way. I love you.

To my beautiful, smart, and funny wife, April, thank you for making me acknowledge that I actually have emotions. You've given me the courage to stand boldly in my truth. You've given me a soft place to land. You've held me in my darkest moments. I love you. Now it's your turn.

To my beloved supporters who pre-ordered this book sight unseen and believed my story was worth reading; I appreciate you. You made this possible, and I'm eternally grateful that you joined me on this journey toward becoming a published author. I appreciate each and every one of you:

Cheryl Stallings

Kimberly Clark

Sumathi Thiyagarajan

Alysha Miller

Trinity Monteiro

Meka Morris

Nicole Britenriker

Alyson McEvoy

Morgan Cato

Liliahn Majeed

Cher Warren

Isioma Nwabuzor

Kori Davis Porter

Eugina Jordan

Cori McKeever

Tony Palomba

Jennifer Almodovar

Kristy Williams

Chelsea Diaz

Kim Washington

Bethany Donaphin

Leah Wilcox

Natoya Brown

Victoria Randle

Natasha Volpe

Deanna Repollet

Tyree White

Brian Levine

Navreet Gill

Travis Apple

Hana Taiji

Lisa Johnson

Amber J. Hutson

Amie Sheridan

Kathy Revelo

Jennifer Martindale

Israel Squires

James Padilla

Erin Schnieders

Dustin Albertson

Heather Hoffman

Sarah Cardon

Bradley Koenen

Edson Crevecoeur

Krista Sinclair

Cassandra Clark

Adam Heintz

Hannah Gordon

Alisha Valavanis

Tahira Ali

Amy Weinfurter

Lindsay Zackon

Kelsey Bannister

Heather Barone

Tara Tallman

Lola Small

Mike Taylor

Mallory LePage

Natalie White

Jamie Weinstein

Ryan Picou

Brandon Lohmann

Whitney Williams

Leonard Edwards

Pamela Noble

Noel Bentley

Jennifer Wilenta

Tracy Billows

Paul Bee

Virginia Mametz

Peter Feigin

Erika Turner

Andrea Knox

Ray Daryabigi

Shelly Finkel

Alexandra Layman

Jackie Chang

Marla Habert

Manju Seal

Brooke Infusino

Alton Byrd

Marcus Madlock

Kevin Brilliant

Cathy Nemerovski

Drew Praster

Monique Lewis

Elijah Frater

Eric Koester

Joe Rugo

Kirk Madsen

Tyshun Wardlaw

Jessica Madison

Kalyn Hutchinson

Maryann Walbert

Cecelia Gore

Maggie Sketch

Maya Flynn

Tony Cartagena

Taylor Flitsch

Hannah Irwin

Evan Contreras

Cale Zomer

I'm beyond grateful for all of you.

APPENDIX

CHAPTER 2

CROWN Coalition. 2023. "CROWN Act Resources — The
Official CROWN Act." The CROWN Act. Accessed October
2, 2022. https://www.thecrownact.com/research-studies.

McCluney, Courtney L. 2021. "The Costs of Code-Switching."
Race (blog), *Harvard Business Review*. January 28, 2021.
https://hbr.org/2019/11/the-costs-of-codeswitching.

CHAPTER 3

Lapchick, Richard L. 2022. *2022 Racial and Gender Report Card.*
Orlando, FL: The Institute for Diversity and Ethics in Sport.

CHAPTER 9

McKay, Adam, director. 2006. *Talladega Nights: The Ballad of
Ricky Bobby*. Columbia Pictures. 1 hr., 48 min.

CHAPTER 10

Ahmed, Idil. 2018. *Manifest Now*. Self-published. Kindle.

CHAPTER 11

Postma, Niven. 2021. "You Can't Sit Out Office Politics." *Office Politics* (blog), *Harvard Business Review*. October 11, 2021. https://hbr.org/2021/07/you-cant-sit-out-office-politics.

CHAPTER 12

McCluney, Courtney L. 2021. "The Costs of Code-Switching." *Race* (blog), *Harvard Business Review*. January 28, 2021. https://hbr.org/2019/11/the-costs-of-codeswitching.

Postma, Niven. 2021. "You Can't Sit Out Office Politics." *Office Politics* (blog), *Harvard Business Review*. October 11, 2021. https://hbr.org/2021/07/you-cant-sit-out-office-politics.

Reardon, Kathleen Kelly. 2001. *The Secret Handshake: Mastering the Politics of the Business Inner Circle.* New York, NY: Currency.

CHAPTER 13

Reardon, Kathleen Kelley. 2015. "Office Politics Isn't Something You Can Sit Out." *Managing Yourself (blog), Harvard Business Review*. January 14, 2015. https://hbr.org/2015/01/office-politics-isnt-something-you-can-sit-out.

Sinek, Simon. 2009. *Start with Why: How Great Leaders Inspire Everyone to Take Action.* New York, NY: Penguin.